The Single Sales Principle
and the 8 Myths of Selling

– MARK BLACKMORE –

An environmentally friendly book printed and bound in England by
www.printondemand-worldwide.com

Mixed Sources
Product group from well-managed
forests, and other controlled sources
www.fsc.org Cert no. TT-COC-002641
© 1996 Forest Stewardship Council

FSC

PEFC
PEFC/16-33-415

PEFC Certified

This product is
from sustainably
managed forests
and controlled
sources

www.pefc.org

This book is made entirely of chain-of-custody materials

FASTPRINT PUBLISHING
PETERBOROUGH, ENGLAND

www.fast-print.net/store.php

THE SINGLE SALES PRINCIPLE
AND THE 8 MYTHS OF SELLING
Copyright © Mark Blackmore 2011

ISBN 978-184426-913-6

First published 2011 by
FASTPRINT PUBLISHING
Peterborough, England.

This book is dedicated to William John Blackmore,
a Single Principled Salesperson.

Thanks to Ala for inspiring the Single Sales Principle,
and to Tim for believing in it.

About the Author

Mark Blackmore is an experienced consultant and passionate sales and management educator. He has worked in a wide variety of sectors and his worldwide clients include Google, Yell, Auto Trader, NHS, Black & Decker, Capita, McAfee, Korn Ferry, Archant, FSS, Opodo, Hellmann Worldwide Logistics and SCA Hygiene.

During 17 highly successful years in sales and sales management he won top performer awards at every organisation for which he worked, including Yellow Pages and The iGate Group.

In 2002 Mark co-founded Lammore Consulting Ltd. Lammore is a training consultancy specialising in developing and delivering innovative sales, leadership and management programmes. The Single Sales Principle® and DECIDE® sales process is now adopted as the methodology of choice by some of the world's leading sales forces.

Lammore's mission is to 'Inspire, Entertain and Make a Difference'. Mark's energetic and entertaining delivery style means that people not only enjoy his seminars, they implement the learning from them. He is a trusted advisor and contributor to the media on sales and leadership related issues, and regularly appears as a guest speaker on the UK's largest conference stages.

Mark is married, with three children and lives in Harrogate, North Yorkshire. He spends the rest of his time marathon running, song writing and being entertained by his young family.

Contents

Introduction

"The great enemy of the truth is very often not the lie - deliberate, contrived and dishonest - but the myth - persistent, persuasive and unrealistic"

John Fitzgerald Kennedy

Selling is the simplest of all professions. This principle follows a simple formula; a single principle. (And there is only one – no matter what the sales gurus will try to tell you.)

It contains just 16 words and will explain unequivocally the mystique of selling. By the end of Chapter 1 you will know what it is.

So why write a book about a principle that can be stated in a simple 16 words?

That's where the 8 myths of selling come in.

12th December 1971

Do you remember how you felt when you discovered there wasn't really a Santa Claus? I remember it well. It was the 12th December 1971 and my (so- called) best friend Johnny Harrison broke the fateful news to me over a Curly Wurly. I felt like I had been had. You don't question what you are told as a kid; you just believe it to be true.

Well, that was also the way I felt the day that I discovered that everything that I had been taught up to that point in sales was a complete lie; all myths. They were theories that had no substance in the modern world. Just catchy phrases that looked good in sales books and on the walls of every hard-core sales office across the land. They were myths that had been taught by well-meaning sales managers, eager to pass on the wisdom and knowledge that their sales managers had passed on to them. But, like a cult, no-one had questioned whether they were true. They may have worked in their day, but they simply do not work today.

And that's the reason for this book. It isn't enough to just preach what should be done. We need to unravel what has gone before.

George Orwell said "He who controls the present, controls the past. He who controls the past, controls the future." To release the future, therefore, we need to understand the past.

Most people know that the dodo was a flightless bird. What is widely unknown is that it was once able to fly. Pre 1600 there were no predators on Mauritius. So, thinking it was a smart thing to do, the dodo decided to conserve energy by giving up the exhausting task of flying. After all, why fly if you don't have to? When Dutch sailors arrived on the island they carried pigs on their ships. Pigs liked the taste of dodos. Within just 80 years the dodo became extinct.

Follow the 8 myths of selling and the end to your sales career will be considerably quicker.

Elvis Is Dead

Walk into most sales offices and you'll see the 8 myths of selling proudly displayed on the wall (probably next to the target and the 'Inspiration' poster):

"Attitude Sets Altitude"

"People Buy People"

"Always Be Closing"

"Customers Like to Talk about Themselves"

"It's a Numbers Game"

"Sell the Sizzle, not the Sausage"

"Money Talks"

"Fail to Plan, Plan to Fail"

Be honest with me. You believe in at least half of the 8 myths yourself, don't you? You are not alone. Most salespeople will quote them as the 'sales gospel'. Suggest that they are myths and they will think you have gone mad.

On the surface the 8 myths look perfectly reasonable. In fact, set inside a picture frame, each one looks positively motivating. And I am sure they made a lot of sense, at the time. Like the dodo, you could be excused for thinking what has worked in the past will work in the future.

But things change. And so has selling.

The 8 myths of selling carry a certain nostalgia, but it is exactly this nostalgia that is wasting your time, reducing your sales performance and costing you money. Elvis is dead, and so are the 8 myths.

This book exposes the 8 myths of selling and introduces a new principle of selling: The Single Sales Principle®; and a new way of selling: the DECIDE® Sales Process.

Part 1
The Single Sales Principle®

Mark Blackmore

Chapter One:
The Search for the Single Sales Principle®

"If you are searching for anything in particular you don't find it, but something falls out at the back that is often more interesting."
JM Barrie (Scottish Writer)

As members of the second oldest profession in the world, salespeople throughout time have developed weird and wonderful theories on how best to sell their wares. Having observed 1000s of sales calls as a salesperson, sales director and sales trainer, I have witnessed at first hand the shortcomings and failure of the 8 myths to deliver. I have watched as well-meaning salespeople become frustrated and disheartened when their best efforts go unrewarded. And in sales, effort counts for nothing. It's all about results.

I guess that's why I love selling. I love its transparency. It is like sport. There is no subjectivity on who is the best. The fastest runner breaks the tape first. The best performer finishes highest above target.

The Top Performer Formula

I have been fortunate enough to have worked with some of the UK's greatest salespeople and my quest to discover 'what makes a top performer' has turned me into a sales voyeur.

But what actually makes an individual better than the rest? What is the magic formula used by top performers? Why is it that top performers will *always* beat the also-rans? They are given the same tools as the also-rans. They have the same products and services as the also-rans. Their territories are demographically aligned with the also-rans. Their sales collateral is issued by the same marketing department as the also-rans. They are allowed to discount to the same percentage as the also-rans. Yet the also-rans are never even in the same league. Top performers always outperform their colleagues...simply always.

The Yellow Pages Best Practice Study

During my time at *Yellow Pages* I was involved in a study to identify the best practice adopted by the company's top salespeople. The purpose of the study was to find a new and improved method of selling that would propel the business into the 21st century. *Yellow Pages* salespeople had for many years been widely regarded as having one of the most highly-trained and disciplined sales forces in the UK. So to have the chance of assessing the best of the best was a great opportunity.

And what did we discover? Well, not what the business was hoping for, that's for sure!

The single most important discovery from the study was that the best salespeople sold in styles that were very different from one another. In fact, pretty much the only thing that they had in common was that they had very little in common!

We did, however, find the following similarities:

1. They were all passionate about the *Yellow Pages* product.

2. Few of them followed the *Yellow Pages* structured sales process.

The first similarity made sense. It is widely accepted that a salesperson needs to believe in the product they are selling. If they do not, their body language betrays their true feelings and the customer sees through it. But there were many other salespeople who had an undying belief in the *Yellow Pages* product at the time, but were only delivering average results. Belief in the product *per se* wasn't the secret ingredient to achieving sales excellence.

The biggest surprise from the survey was the top performers' lack of use of the YP sales process. And it was the sales process that we all believed was the secret ingredient. But it wasn't. We were confused.

The Search Continued

I left the company shortly after the study and, thinking that maybe the *Yellow Pages* situation was a one-off, I continued my quest to identify 'the top performer formula' by observing the best salespeople from some of the world's leading organisations in my role as a sales trainer.

And what was my conclusion? It was just the same! None of them followed a standard sales process. They certainly didn't follow the 8 myths of selling. Yet again, it was pretty much the only thing they had in common. Indeed, it was the one thing that differentiated them from everyone else.

Knowing what they didn't do hadn't got me any closer to discovering what they *did* do. The more I studied top performers, the more frustrated I became.

The Discovery of the Single Sales Principle®

I then realised I had been looking in the wrong direction. As J.M Barrie promised, as I was looking for one thing, something much more interesting fell out the back! As a sales trainer I had always assessed a salesperson's ability to implement a sales process. It was all about the salesperson: how they opened up the sale; how they identified needs; how they presented their products; how they closed the sale. And this was exactly the problem.

The eureka moment was when I realised that:

Great salespeople are customer-centric, not sales-centric.

It was the one thing that all top performers shared. Instead of following a rigid sales process, they spent their energies on ensuring that a customer was guided through the buying cycle. They ensured that a customer had all of the ingredients required to make a purchasing decision. They focused on how the customer was relating to the product. In short, top performers were 'externally focused', not 'internally focused'.

Here's a quick test to illustrate what I mean.

Think of the capital version of the letter 'q' and draw it on your forehead using your index finger. Which way is the tail pointing? To the left or right? If it is to the right you have drawn it introspectively, i.e. as if *you* were reading it. You are not alone. Most people view the world with an internal focus.

If the tail points to the left you have drawn it with an external perspective, i.e. as if someone else was reading it.

Don't worry! This exercise doesn't qualify you in or out as a Single Principled Salesperson. But it is worth reflecting on where your primary thought process is centred.

Historical step-by-step sales methods focus on the salesperson's actions. They are created to extract what they want from the customer. As do the 8 myths. Each one was created for the benefit of the salesperson, not the customer.

It was clear that the secret to sales success lay with the buyer, not the seller. The search continued.

60 Second Summary:
The Search for the Single Sales Principle®

Great Salespeople are customer-centric, not sales-centric.

They focus on the key components that help a customer make a purchasing decision.

It's all about the buyer, not the seller.

Chapter Two:
The Single Sales Principle®

"In matters of style, swim with the current; in matters of principle, stand like a rock."

Thomas Jefferson

Based on the discovery that Top Performers are customer-centric, not sales-centric, my business partner at Lammore Consulting, Tim Haslam, and I decided to take a different tack. Instead of studying salespeople (our approach up until then) we focused on the customer. What were the reasons people buy and, just as importantly, what prevented them from making a purchase?

We commissioned *One-Poll* to survey a wide range of people from varying demographic groups. The results were emphatic. Emphatically obvious! So obvious in fact we wondered how we missed it:

The reasons people gave for *not* making a purchase included:

- "The salesperson didn't understand my needs"

- "The salesperson didn't understand his product"
- "I felt too pressurised"
- "The price I was quoted was too high"
- "The salesperson didn't come back to me"

The reasons people gave *for* making a purchase included:

- "The product ticked all of my boxes"
- "The product looked great"
- "I trusted the brand"
- "It was good value"
- "I liked the colour"

Notice anything about the two lists? The reasons people didn't buy all featured the *salesperson*, whereas the reasons why they did buy all focused on the *product*. It taught us that salespeople are like wigs...you only notice the bad ones! Great salespeople are able to sell without the customer realising they are being sold to.

Using the *One Poll* survey we were able to identify the key elements that have to be present for an individual to make a purchase. It wasn't difficult. There were three clearly definable components that kept emerging in successful sales, and were missing in unsuccessful sales. Not sometimes, but always.

We soon realised that, like a chemical equation, they followed a simple formula; a fundamental principle. And no matter which way we looked at it, it always came back to this single principle. This is why we called it the ***Single Sales Principle®***.

Here it is:

People buy when a Compelling Need is met by a Credible Solution that offers Perceived Value.

This is the single most important principle of selling. Let's see it again:

People buy when a *Compelling Need* is met by a *Credible Solution* that offers *Perceived Value*

Or if you want to see it in a mathematical equation:

Compelling Need + Credible Solution + Perceived Value = People Buy

Or if you work better with graphics (see Figure 1):

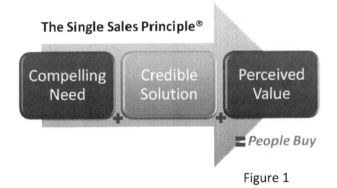

Figure 1

If you achieve the Single Sales Principle® in every sales call, I promise that you will never lose a sale again! I also guarantee that every sale you didn't make was because you *didn't* deliver the Single Sales Principle®.

Simple.

Too simple? Well, as Jim Collins claims in his book *Good to Great*, "Freud, Darwin and Einstein all had one thing in common. They took a complex world and simplified it." And Single Principled Salespeople do just that. They understand that selling doesn't have to be complicated. They simply make it easy for a customer to buy.

Billy Wright was the first footballer from any nation to win a century of international caps and still holds the record for captaining England 90 times. I love his philosophy on defending: "I only had two things on my mind: to win the ball and then give the simplest pass I could to the nearest team-mate." Simple.

Winston Churchill said "Out of intense complexities, simplicities emerge." Selling has become a complicated business. But it doesn't have to be. Don't be fooled. Simple is good.

For those of you that live your life in headlines, feel free to put this book down (unless you're still in the bookshop!) because you've just read the most important part of the book. In fact, I firmly believe that the Single Sales Principle® is the most important 16 words that you will ever read in your selling careers.

For the rest that need a little more explanation however (and I am assuming that is most of us), please read on.

The Single Sales Principle® Explained

The Single Sales Principle®: People buy when a Compelling Need is met by a Credible Solution that offers Perceived Value.

1. Compelling Need

A compelling need is made up of 2 factors:

a) The Need

A customer must have a need for your product or service. Needs are fundamental to selling as no-one buys anything unless they have a need.

A need can be a problem to be solved, or a desire to be achieved. They can be emotionally motivated (e.g. peace of mind, prestige) or rationally motivated (e.g. profit, cost-based).

Despite popular belief, even the greatest salespeople in the world can't sell if there isn't a need. If a salesperson has sold 'sand to the Arabs' it was because the Arab needed it. As did the Eskimo who bought ice. We can argue over what the need would have been, but there definitely would have been one.

b) Compelling Reason for Action

The need must be compelling enough to motivate the customer into taking action. Just having a need is not enough to drive change. Only if the need is compelling will the individual make the purchase.

The other day our dishwasher broke. We had a definite need to replace it, but we didn't rush out and buy one. Why not? Because it was easier to wash the dishes by hand than go to the hassle of replacing the old one. After spending an hour at the sink washing up after a family Sunday lunch, however, we decided it was time to get down to our local electrical store! We were now motivated into action.

So what happens if the compelling need is missing?

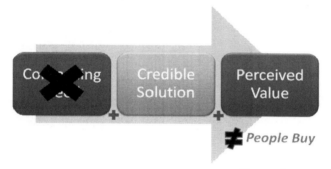

Figure 2

You deliver a credible solution and the customer perceives that it is good value, but the result is 'No Sale'.

It's like being the best-looking guy in the nightclub, but the girl you're chatting up is happily married and not looking for love! You win brownie points for offering a good value proposition, but you are not going to close this deal.

2. Credible Solution

Credible solutions are also made up of two ingredients:

a) Credibility

Why you? Will you/the product actually deliver on the promise? What reassurance can you offer? Do you have the relevant qualifications? Who else have you worked with?

b) The Solution

Will the solution actually meet my specific needs? Has the proposal been presented in a clear and understandable way?

So what happens if the credible solution is missing?

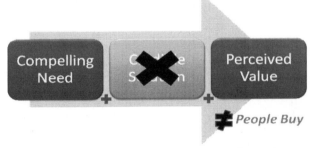

Figure 3

Your customer has a compelling need and you are offering perceived value, but again the result is 'No Sale'.

The girl you are chatting up in the nightclub is looking for a new man in her life, and you have tried to woo her with offers of champagne and caviar. Sadly for you, however, she is not impressed with your corny lines, 80s outfit and current vocation. You need to work seriously on your proposition; because she is definitely going to choose someone, it just won't be you!

3. Perceived Value

Perceived value occurs when the compelling need and credible solution (i.e. the solution match) are aligned with the price.

So how is value judged?

Imagine I have a compelling need to buy orange juice. Compare the price of the following ways of buying the same brand of orange juice?

- In a carton from a snack van: £1
- In a glass from a *Wetherspoon* pub: £2
- In a champagne flute from *The Ritz* hotel: £5

In this scenario all of the solutions offer value for money because the perception of value is determined by the credible solution.

You may feel that £5 is excessive for an orange juice. There are, however, some important business contacts at *The Ritz* business networking event. In this scenario £5 is worth the investment because your compelling need to network has made it value for money.

So what happens if the perceived value is missing?

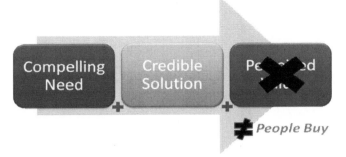

Figure 4

Back in the nightclub. You have perfectly matched the girl's compelling need with your credible solution, but you expected her to pick up the tab for the bubbly, and she decided the bill didn't justify the relationship!

60 Second Summary:
The Single Sales Principle®

The Single Sales Principle®: People buy when a *compelling need* is met by a *credible solution* that offers *perceived value*.

1. Compelling Need
Compelling needs are made up of two ingredients:

a) Need
Customer must have a need for your product or service. Needs are fundamental to selling as no-one buys anything unless they have a need.

b) Compelling Reason for Action
This need must be compelling enough to motivate them towards action.

2. Credible Solution
Credible solutions are made up of two ingredients:

a) Credibility
Why should I listen to you? Will you/the product actually deliver on the promise?

b) The Solution
Will the solution be clearly demonstrated in a way that convinces me that it will meet my specific needs?

3. Perceived Value
Perceived value is determined by aligning price with the compelling need and the credible solution (i.e. the solution match).

Mark Blackmore

Chapter Three:
The Single Principled
Salesperson

"Bond is an enigma. He's smooth and bigger than life, but he's vague as a personality."

Pierce Brosnan (Actor who played 007)

Jim Collins defined great leaders as 'Level 5' leaders in *Good to Great.* A Level 5 leader, he wrote, displays a "paradoxical blend of personal humility and professional will inspiring others via inspired standards – excellence, hard work and integrity, not with an inspiring charismatic persona." The same can very often be said of Single Principled Salespeople.

Spotting a Single Principled Salesperson in a crowd is a challenge because they just don't look or sound like salespeople. Think of a typical salesperson and you imagine a confident, loud, 'life and soul of the party' type of person.

Single Principled Salespeople, however, come in a range of guises. Some are gregarious, some are withdrawn. Some put in the hours. Some stroll to victory. Some are process-driven; some go with the flow.

Single Principled Salespersons often behave like mavericks. They frequently rebel against the company line because they don't follow the prescribed processes and scripts. To the untrained eye their sales approach may come across as unconventional. But when analysed, there is a common thread that runs through every one of their sales calls: they all follow the Single Sales Principle®.

Are You a Single Principled Salesperson?

As discussed, it is not easy to spot a Single Principled Salesperson through their appearance. The easiest way of spotting a Single Principled Salesperson is to take a look at the sales numbers! As the Olympian, Michael Johnson, once said, "They don't give you gold medals for beating somebody. They give you gold medals for beating everybody."

The Single Principled Salesperson is quite simply head and shoulders above their peers in terms of performance. They are the undisputed top performer in the company. They know it. Their colleagues know it. Their bosses know it. Their customers know it.

The last point is particularly important to the Single Principled Salesperson as they are evangelical about the customer. This is because the customer is at the core of the Single Sales Principle®. If the organisation does not provide effective solutions that meet the customer's needs, the Single Principled Salesperson cannot justify the sale. The Single Sales Principle® is incomplete and the result is lose-lose for both parties.

That is why they are often outspoken when internal policies affect external performance. They believe that problems are not opportunities. Problems are problems. And problems need to be sorted. In meetings, they will often be seen challenging the status quo and forever looking for ways to improve performance. This means that the Single Principled Salesperson is unpopular at times as they often ruffle a few too many feathers.

Unpopular, that is except in the eyes of their sales manager! The Single Principled Salesperson never misses a target. Simply never. And they consistently raise the bar.

We all know a Single Principled Salesperson. They may not be as popular as the other guys in the team, but we all know which one we aspire to be.

The Others in the Sales Team

To help us in our quest to discover the truth about the 8 myths of selling I have commissioned two other salespeople to give their philosophies on selling: 'Ronnie the Rep', and 'Textbook Tarquin.' You will recognise Ronnie and Tarquin,as they are in every sales team you have ever worked within.

Ronnie the Rep

Ronnie the Rep has been a salesman all his life. He is a 'Rough Diamond.' You know the type. He has been around forever, and seen many come, try, and fail. He loves the salesman's life: the car; the expense allowance; the first meeting at 10.30am; the last meeting at 3pm. He believes that business is conducted on the golf course, which is where you'll find him most Friday afternoons.

He'll talk to anyone; anyone who will care to listen. Not that there is a shortage of a willing audience. Ronnie is funny. We all love Ronnie. His stories about life on the road keep us entertained for hours. Ronnie's suit may look a little tired, and his tie may sit uncomfortably around his unbuttoned collar, but Ronnie is the spokesman for the journeyman salesperson. Selling has been a way of life for Ronnie, and has provided him with a good living. He won't admit it, but each month is getting more of a struggle. To hit his targets he needs to use every trick in the book. But hit he normally does. Despite the targets getting tougher, he'll do just enough to get himself over the line. When all's said and done, he's an asset to the team. His lack of finesse is more than compensated for by his character.

We all know a Ronnie. We wish we were as funny as him. We respect him for staying the course. At the same time we pray that we don't turn out like him. We hope that by the time we get to Ronnie's age we would have moved on...somewhere...anywhere but here.

Textbook Tarquin

Textbook Tarquin is the antipathy of Ronnie. He is always the first one in the office, and the last one to leave. He came top of the training course and carries around his sales manual like a Bible. When he prepares for a meeting no stone is left unturned, and no website is left un-surfed. He wears a plain, smart, civil-servant-style suit and his hair is 'short back and sides'.

Textbook Tarquin is the sort of guy that girls feel safe taking home to mum. Clients also like him. Why wouldn't they? In front of a customer he is the consummate professional. The trainers on the induction programme took a video of him selling because he sells just the way they train it. He is the rare species that actually uses the sales PowerPoint presentation created by the marketing department. His meetings are rarely less than two hours, because that's how long a textbook sale takes. By the end of the sales process the customer may not buy, but they will feel he represented his organisation well. His bosses like him because he is hard-working and honest.

He places a high emphasis on efficiency, and is never late with his call sheets, expenses, or updating the CRM system. Textbook Tarquin's sales performance is solid; not spectacular, but solid. His lack of natural flair is compensated for by his commitment to and belief in the sales method. We admire his dedication. We wish we were as organised and had his attention to detail. But it all seems too unnatural in Textbook Tarquin's world and we can't help but think there must be a better way.

There is. It's the Single Sales Principle®. In Part 2, I will show you how to implement the Single Sales Principle® using the DECIDE® Sales Process. Each step of DECIDE® is specifically aligned to meeting the 3 key elements of the Single Sales Principle®.

60 Second Summary:
The Single Principled Salesperson

Single Principled Salespeople come in a range of guises. The easiest way of spotting a Single Principled Salesperson is to take a look at their sales numbers. The Single Principled Salesperson never misses a target. They consistently raise the bar.

Despite their differences they all have the following in common:

- they are passionate about their product/service
- they are vocal when the company does not deliver for the customer
- they never follow the 8 myths
- they all follow the Single Sales Principle®

Mark Blackmore

Part Two
How to Implement the Single Sales Principle® : DECIDE®

Mark Blackmore

Chapter 1:
The DECIDE® Sales Process

Exposing Sales Myth #1:
ABC - Always Be Closing

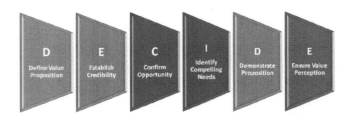

"I am the world's worst salesman…. I must make it easy for people to buy."

Gene Fowler (American Journalist)

Ronnie the Rep:

"If a salesperson isn't closing, they're not selling. I know every type of close ever written, and a few more besides! I once used the pressure of silence on a close and stared the customer out for 10 minutes! We both knew that whoever 'broke and spoke' first would lose. Needless to say, the customer buckled!

I am closing the minute the prospect picks up the phone. Each close gets me closer to the "yes", and each "yes" gets me closer to signing the deal."

Textbook Tarquin:

"Hard selling is not really my forte. I follow the sales process, steps to handling an objection, and various closes as per our company sales manual, but they don't always work. I seem to lose the customer somewhere."

The Single Principled Salesperson:

"If you need to use closing techniques to get a sale, you clearly haven't demonstrated that your product meets their needs. Rather than force the customer into a decision they undoubtedly will regret, I simply go back to where I lost them in the buying process, and start again from there. If you apply the Single Sales Principle® you don't need to close...the customer should be asking you to buy."

Coffee is for Closers

The American Journalist Gene Fowler said "I am the world's worst salesman…. I must make it easy for people to buy." I reckon Gene was a Single Principled Salesperson, because Single Principled Salespeople always makes it easy for a customer to 'DECIDE®'.

'Always Be Closing' is the ultimate sales myth. Its place was cemented in sales folklore by its appearance in the film *Glengarry Glen Ross*. Alec Baldwin plays a tough-talking area manager from downtown, and goes into an underperforming real estate sales team to read the riot act. The film also coins the now infamous line 'Coffee is for Closers', where a down-on-his-luck journeyman sales guy played by Jack Lemmon is told he isn't allowed the privilege of free office coffee as he hadn't closed any business that month.

I often show this particular scene to sales teams and without fail it brings out the macho side of every salesperson in the room. The unanimous view of the delegates is that 'closing is selling', and if you can't close, you can't sell.

This theory was examined in great depth by Neil Rackham in his book *SPIN Selling*. Rackham also found that the ability to close and negotiate was perceived by salespeople and managers alike as the most important skill in selling. His subsequent research, however, challenged this theory. Rackham discovered that the use of closing techniques had no influence on the success or otherwise of a large sale.

Despite Rackham's evidence, however, the perception of the sales community hasn't changed. Like the Santa myth maybe we don't want to know the truth, because years after *SPIN*

Selling was written, 'negotiation' still ranks as the highest keyword entered into *Google* by desperate salespeople and sales managers looking for 'the secret to success' (see Figure 5).

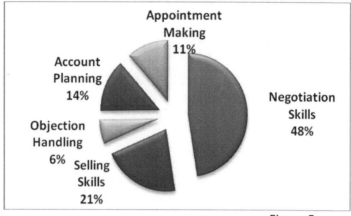

Figure 5

In my early years selling double glazing we would boast about our closing techniques like kids comparing World Cup stickers. Sure we all knew the Alternative Close, the Direct Close and the Assumptive Close. Everyone had these closes in their album and they had no swap value whatsoever. The more notorious, and downright dishonest the closes were, the more kudos the closer achieved. I cringe at some of the 'scams' that my colleagues used when trying to close a sale: the answer-phone close; the first-night-only-discount close; the Benjamin Franklin close (pros and cons).

Our sales manager for the window company was a big ominous Scotsman who spoke like Taggart and acted like there really had been a murder. He would encourage us to swap our tales from the night before, as it was good for morale. Once the meeting had finished, 'Taggart' would call us into his office one by one. At this point you would be told whether or not the business had 'stuck' from the night before. The government had recently introduced the 'customer cooling-off period' and many of the deals sold would be cancelled the following day. 'Taggart' wasn't happy about this new law. "It's killing the art of selling", he would grumble. In his opinion we had done our job as we 'sold' it, despite the cancellation.

But looking back, I strongly disagree. We hadn't done our jobs. If we had, they wouldn't have cancelled.

Here's the point:

Great salespeople don't need to close. They simply help a customer to DECIDE®.

Back in the 'old days' of sales the time spent at various stages of a sale mirrored a triangle (see Figure 6).

Figure 6

At the top of the triangle we 'talk about you', but only superficially. "Where did you go on your holiday?" may often be the extent of the fact find. This quickly turns into "let me tell you everything there is to know about me!" Feature after feature is propelled towards the customer, regardless of whether they are interested or not. Finally, we close, and we close hard, using every technique in the book.

I was trained in this way of selling by a notoriously hard-sell, highly- priced vacuum cleaner manufacturer. We spent very little time in the fact find. There was no need to ask any questions as we had no real interest in what the customer's needs were. We were only interested in demonstrating the benefits of the vacuum cleaner. So we went straight to the middle of the triangle and delivered a well-rehearsed pitch about all of the different attachments, speeds and usages.

The presentation took exactly 18 minutes and by the end we had given them so much information you would believe the cleaner could be launched into space. The fact that most people didn't need all of the extra features was irrelevant to us. Our belief was they would be so impressed they'd want it anyway.

Finally came the fun bit: the close. As the price was 10 times the price of a standard vacuum cleaner we needed a number of manipulative closes to get the person to sign. But sign they would. We were double-hard salespeople, and proud of it!

Since the advent of consultative selling, however, buyers now expect to be involved in the purchase much more. They will buy only if they feel that the salesperson has understood their needs, and can prove the value of their product in meeting those needs. The triangle theory still applies, only this time it is inverted (see Figure 7).

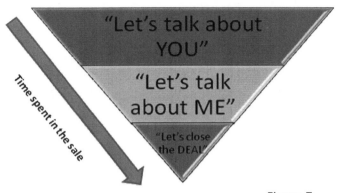

Figure 7

The fact find ("let's talk about you") is now at the widest part of the triangle and, as such, demands the most amount of time to be spent upon it. The salesperson needs to identify exactly what the customer is looking for, why they are looking for it, how badly they need it, and what would happen if they didn't get it. Only once this has been established can the salesperson offer their solution ("let's talk about me"), because only then do they know the issues their product has to solve.

Finally: the close. If the process has been customer-centric, the buyer should be asking the salesperson how to proceed, not the other way round. We call this Win-Win. The salesperson has won, because they got the order, and the customer has won because they got something that was right for them. In the good old/bad old days we used to pride ourselves on Win-Lose. We got the deal but at what cost? The customer woke up the next morning, got 'buyer's remorse', and cancelled. Win-Lose invariably turned into

Lose-Lose because we lost our order and commission, and they lost out on new windows/vacuum cleaner, etc.

The DECIDE® Sales Process

So how do you achieve the Single Sales Principle® through a customer-centric approach? The answer is by using the DECIDE® sales process.

Dr. W. Edwards Deming convinced the world of the importance of process whilst turning around the fortune of post-war Japan. Through the concept of 'Total Quality' he demonstrated the power of systems, stating: "94% of failures are not because the person didn't want to do a good job........it's the system that failed."

Single Principled Salespeople are customer-centric and appreciate that guiding a customer through the Single Sales Principle® is fundamental to making a sale.

Figure 8 shows the alignment between the Single Sales Principle® and DECIDE®. Each step of DECIDE® is specifically designed to meet the key elements of the Single Sales Principle®.

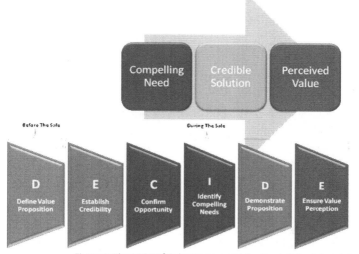

Figure 8: The DECIDE® Sales Process and the Single Sales Principle®

The DECIDE® Sales Process: Overview

1. Define Value Proposition

The first part of the sales process occurs prior to meeting the customer. Its purpose is to define your value proposition, specifically for the client you are about to meet/call.

2. Establish Credibility

Engaging with the prospect is vital to gaining their attention and interest. This is achieved by establishing your credibility early on in the sales call.

3. Confirm Opportunity

To make a recommendation there is certain information that must be obtained from the customer. A Single Principled Salesperson will establish the size of the opportunity ensuring that they maximise their sales time.

4. Identify Compelling Needs

Needs must be identified prior to presenting the proposition. Single Principled Salespeople also test the importance of the need, identifying whether the need will motivate the buyer into action.

5. Demonstrate Proposition

The proposition is demonstrated by matching the credible solution to the customer's compelling needs in a dynamic way.

6. Ensure Value Perception

The deal is closed when the customer appreciates the perceived value of the proposition. This occurs when the price is in line with the solution match (compelling need/credible solution). If the Single Sales Principle® has been achieved this should be simple as the customer is now ready to buy.

60 Second Summary:
The DECIDE® Sales Process

Great salespeople don't need to close. They simply help a customer to *DECIDE®*.

Single Principled Salespeople spend more time asking questions than they do talking about their product or service. In doing so the close is simply a case of agreeing next steps.

In satisfying the Single Sales Principle®, Single Principled Salespeople follow the DECIDE® sales process when helping a buyer make a purchasing decision.

The DECIDE® Sales Process:

1. Define Value Proposition
2. Establish Credibility
3. Confirm Opportunity
4. Identify Compelling Needs
5. Demonstrate Proposition
6. Ensure Value Perception

Chapter Two:
Define Value Proposition

Exposing Sales Myth #2:
Attitude Sets Altitude

"How many legs does a dog have if you call the tail a leg?
Four. Calling a tail a leg doesn't make it a leg".
Abraham Lincoln

Ronnie the Rep:

"Every morning I wake up, go into the bathroom, look at myself in the mirror, and scream 10 times 'you're a winner!' I then dress to impress – always fully suited and booted. If I didn't want to wear a tie I'd have become a roofer. If I look good on the outside, I feel good on the inside. I imagine the customer is holding my Mont Blanc pen in his hand and is signing the order. That's why I'm successful – I believe in myself. When Ronnie the Rocket is in town, the customer is putty in his hands."

Textbook Tarquin:

"I am not what you would call a natural salesperson. I sometimes think I have a bit too much empathy for the customer. Our products are a lot of money and market conditions are tough for our customers right now. And our competitors offer very cost-effective solutions. Maybe I am a bit too honest. People sometimes call me negative. I just think I am being a realist."

The Single Principled Salesperson:

"No amount of telling myself that I'm a tiger will work if I don't believe in my product and that comes from a deep, genuine belief in whether I am delivering the Single Sales Principle®. The better my value proposition, the more positive I am. If I am negative it is because I see a weakness in my credible solution, a lack of compelling needs or no perceived value. Rather than waste time doing star-jumps in the office, I re-energise myself by focusing on the Single Sales Principle®. Once I get that right everything else just fits into place.

You're a Tiger

Ever attended one of those 'Believe in Yourself' courses? I have. My boss thought it would be good for team-building. Our morale was low and sales were even lower. The first thing that bothered me when we entered the room was the lack of tables. Instead of chairs we had bean bags. The guy running the course was friendly enough, although you could tell that he had wrestled with his dress code – like a politician wearing jeans, his attempt at 'smart casual' hadn't quite worked.

He spoke about anything being possible; you can always get what you want; all you need is the power of positive thinking. He told us his life story. How he was bankrupt. How he had no job, no partner, no self-esteem. Yet through the power of positive thinking he now has it all, in abundance. He didn't say how much, but he implied it was much more than we had. He set up an exercise. We were to think of what we wanted to achieve – no limits.

"Anything?", I asked.

"Yes, anything", he replied.

I decided I wouldn't be greedy and asked for a multi-million pound annual income; Claudia Schiffer during the week and Cheryl Cole at weekends; and world peace to round things off.

We had to close our eyes and imagine we had achieved our goals right now. Feel it. Believe it. I'm not sure whether the earth moved for Claudia, but all I could think about was how painful my backside was - Zen thinking is tough in a conference room in Slough, no matter how strategically the bean bags are placed.

At the end of the session, he gave us all a positive affirmation tape which was to be played at least three times a day. The American on the tape (why are they always American?) said a motivational line and we had to repeat it, with 'feeling'.

"I believe in myself";

"I can achieve my ultimate destiny";

"I am a tiger".

Now there is only one person I am aware of who can call himself 'tiger'. And if you've seen my golf swing you would know that no amount of roaring in front of the mirror is going to turn me into him.

Our boss was delighted with the day. At the beginning of each day thereafter he would play the tape and get us to repeat it out loud as a group. Bearing in mind I was one of the keen ones, even I thought that he had lost the plot this time. The older guys in the office paid lip service, and then ripped it apart once the boss had left the room.

But I gave it a genuine attempt. Sales were so bad I was prepared to try anything. But the results didn't get better, they got worse. And this was the reason why.

Our value proposition was rubbish!

It was a good product 5 years ago. In fact 5 years ago it had turned a small U.S. business into a multinational organisation employing 7000 people. But times had changed and what was good then wasn't good anymore. Worse still – no-one had the initiative, gumption, or the balls to say so.

Nobody had a clue how our product actually worked, preventing us from identifying what was good about it. This made it pretty difficult to work out why someone should buy the thing.

Doublethink

I didn't realise it at the time, but scientific research has proven that just sitting in a room visualising success is paramount to ensuring that you will fail.

A study at the University of Pennsylvania by Gabriele Oettingen showed that students who 'dreamed' of their perfect job once they graduated actually received fewer job offers and had significantly smaller salaries than those who were prepared for the rocky road ahead.

Professor Richard Wiseman in his book *59 Seconds* writes "In *Nineteen Eighty-Four*, George Orwell introduced the concept of Doublethink, describing it as the simultaneous holding of two opposing beliefs in one's mind and yet accepting both."

Identifying why someone should buy your product and, conversely, why they wouldn't buy it, is essential to creating a value proposition.

Here's the point:

A genuine belief in your value proposition sets your altitude.

A positive mental attitude comes from a deep, genuine belief in your value proposition. No amount of positive thinking is going to turn a bad product into a good one.

Being positive didn't help General Custer win the Battle of Little Bighorn. There were just too many Indians. Being positive didn't help England score more penalties than the Germans in Italy '90 or Euro '96. The Germans were just better penalty-takers than the English. Being positive didn't stop IBM losing their way towards the end of the last century. 'Big Blue' just didn't realise that software, not hardware, was the real money-spinner.

I am consistently amazed at how many companies just don't understand their value proposition. Yet they invest in motivational speakers to inject enthusiasm into their sales team, hoping a positive mental attitude will see them through. It won't.

By the way, being positive didn't help the American on the tape either. I found out a little while ago he had gone bankrupt, again. So much for positive thinking.

Keeping it Real

"Most passport pictures are good likenesses, and it is time we faced it".

Katharine Brush (US Author)

But if it is all about the product, how come salespeople perform at different levels within the same organisation? Quite simply it is their level of *belief* in the product that affects their altitude. Single Principled Salespeople focus on their value proposition, building belief in why a customer should buy their product.

But it isn't a blind faith. They will also understand the product's shortcomings, and how to deal with them. Through the art of 'doublethink' they prepare a value proposition that is robust and believable. And once a Single Principled Salesperson believes in something, the sky's the limit.

Sun Tzu said "Know yourself and you will win all battles".

Great salespeople understand this philosophy and thrive upon it. Understanding strengths and capitalising on them also defines great companies.

Gillette is one of the great corporate success stories of our generation. They identified that to be the best they had to understand what they were the best at. Gillette recognised that it had two main strengths: the ability to manufacture billions of low-cost, high-tolerant products, and the ability to build global consumer brands. This belief in their ability enabled them to conquer the shaving world and become the 'Coca Cola' of razors.

I love watching new salespeople in their few first weeks in a job. I call it 'rookie enthusiasm'. They believe in the company, and believe in the product. That's why they joined. At first, they smash their targets because all they know are the good things that they were told in the interview and on the induction. They haven't had an order cancel, or a deal messed up by accounts. Their commission hasn't been miscalculated, and their target hasn't been jacked-up unfairly because their colleagues underperformed. And fundamentally, they haven't made enough calls to hear all of the reasons why their product isn't as good as they first thought.

Catching Crabs

All of that starts to change as they start to hang around with the bigger lads behind the bike sheds and get told all the things that are wrong with the job.

My school sports teacher used to say, "If you want to fly like an eagle, don't mix with turkeys."

Ever watched crabs caught by kids in a seaside rock pool? In the bucket they start to demonstrate many characteristics of the sales journeyman. As one tries to escape from the bucket the others drag them back down. An underperforming salesperson feels comforted that they are not the only one missing target. It means they can blame their failures on anything but themselves. They blame the marketplace, the economy, the customer, the pricing policy, the accounts department. As they do so, they pull their fellow crabs further down into the bucket by telling them how tough it is out there.

I hate it when people say "I'm not being negative, I'm just being realistic". No you are not. Invariably you are just being negative.

So what is the difference between 'being realistic' and 'keeping it real?'

It's a state of mind. When people say 'I'm just being realistic' they have typically resigned themselves to defeat.

When people 'keep it real' they appreciate the situation for what it is (both good and bad), and focus on how they can make it better.

Differentiation

"Insanity: doing the same thing over and over again and expecting different results."

Albert Einstein

Woolworths didn't 'keep it real' and clearly didn't listen to Einstein, as despite profits consistently dropping over the last 50 years they carried on doing the same old thing. In the 1960s Woolworths had a thousand stores. In 2009 they declared themselves bankrupt.

So what did Woolworths actually specialise in? CDs and DVDs? Clothes? Toys and Games? Mops and Buckets? Pick 'n' mix? Woolworths were the archetypal jacks of all trades, but masters of none. And there lay the problem. They stopped adding value to the customer.

People stopped wanting what Woolworths had to offer and the absolute bottom line is that you don't need positive mental attitude sessions if people want what you have to sell.

Jack Trout got it spot on in his book *Differentiate or Die*:

"In 1996 Peter Drucker defined Leadership when he wrote 'The foundation of good leadership is thinking through the organisation's mission, defining it and establishing it, clearly and visibly'. We believe that you need to replace *mission* with *difference*."

Mark Blackmore

Having a sexy mission statement may look good in the corporate brochure. But knowing what truly differentiates your product from your competitors' is the key to building a belief in your value proposition.

So what is *your* value proposition? Take a moment please and write it down here:

_____

_____

_____

_____

_____

_____

_____

_____

OK, now that you've done that, please cross it out. It's rubbish!

Why? Well, the likelihood is that it will be bland, uninspiring and totally ineffective.

Of course, some of you would have nailed it; the Single Principled Salespeople amongst you! But the vast majority will be a waste of time and effort. Most salespeople we work with initially come out with lines such as:

'We offer great value to our customers whilst delivering exceptional service';

'Our products are a cost-effective solution to the needs of our buyers'.

'We are simply the best.'

Blah Blah Blah...! The problem with all of these is that they do not *differentiate* you from your competitors. Your competitors are saying that too.

Selling Hope

Some large corporate companies get their marketing teams to be very creative about their proposition. For example:

Kodak: 'We make memories';

Disney – 'We make people happy';

L'Oreal – 'We sell hope'.

My personal favourite is Harley Davidson, whose CEO Jeff Bleustein once stated at a conference that "Harley Davidson make it possible for middle-aged accountants to wear leathers and look tough." Genius!

These slogans served the companies well in adapting and capitalising on a changing world. For example, it helped Kodak's transition from print into new media technology by ensuring they focused on the business of creating memories, whatever the format. It also ensured that Walt Disney established itself as an entertainment business, not just a film-maker.

As slogans they are catchy and explain the brand concept. But I suggest they are created by marketing people for marketing people. As a sales tool they are ineffective and, dare I say it, corny.

I would hazard a guess that Kodak's number one salesperson doesn't walk into a camera shop and expect to impress the buyer with 'we make memories.' The Single Principled Salespeople at Kodak will need to deliver clear, unambiguous *differentiators*, not catchphrases.

Creating a Value Proposition

A product or service only exists if it fulfils a need. Shoes exist to protect our feet. Sunscreen exists to block out the sun. A cup exists to hold liquid.

A pretty simple theory.

So why is it that salespeople feel the need to talk in jargon? When I ask salespeople on seminars what they sell I get answers like:

"We sell CPA to B2B";

"We sell front-to-back-end enterprise solutions";

"We sell contingent services."

What on earth are they talking about?!

When you are asked at a dinner party what you do, do you explain it succinctly and in a way that makes the person want to know more? Or do they pretend to need the loo in an attempt to make a fast getaway?

Or, put another way, when you tell your mother what you sell, does she get it? If the answer is no, then I promise you your dear old mum isn't the only one who is struggling with your proposition.

So how do you create a value proposition? (see Figure 9)

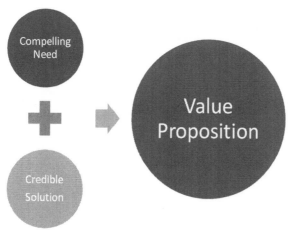

Figure 9

Defining a value proposition is pretty simple. Just take the customer's most compelling need, and explain how you solve it better than anyone else, i.e. your credible solution.

For example, imagine you run a computer repair company. A compelling need could be that people don't want to be without their computers for too long. Your solution is that you fix the computer at the customer's office or home. Your value proposition therefore could be:

"We are PC and laptop repair specialists. The difference with us is that we come to you, meaning that you don't have the inconvenience of being without your computer."

Imagine you owned a sandwich shop. The compelling need of your customers may be that they only have one hour for lunch and do not want to spend it waiting in line. Your solution may be a 'call-ahead service.' In which case your value proposition could be:

"We sell freshly-prepared sandwiches. The key difference with us is we reduce waiting times by allowing you to phone us with your order in advance."

But what if you need further inspiration in identifying your value proposition? This can be achieved by looking at your Proposition Concept and Proposition Edge. (see Figure 10)

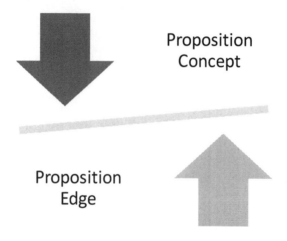

Figure 10

1. The Proposition Concept

The Proposition Concept explains what it is that you do, and why it is a better way of doing it than other methods you could choose. It doesn't explain why you are better at it than your competitors. That is the role of the Proposition Edge.

To explain, imagine we wanted to set up an online dating agency that specialises in meeting the needs of the busy, high-earning executive. Let's call the service *'Love Finder.'* The proposition concept is 'online dating'.

Some people still do not buy into online dating so we need to sell the benefits of meeting someone on the internet rather than via other ways, such as speed-dating, nightclubbing and leaving it to chance.

The following table helps to define the proposition concept:

How else could you find romance	What's the problem with this way?	Why do it your way?
Meet someone through everyday life e.g. work, gym, bus stop	Left to chance Difficult to find the right match Shyness gets in the way	More proactive approach Refined search - only meet people who suit your criteria Confidential – no embarrassment
Go to night clubs	Get people with wrong intentions Intimidating environment Safety risk	Selection Criteria - get people with right 'intentions' Online - not intimidating Comfort of own home – safer
Speed-dating	False situation – too fast Don't get to know person Feeling of rejection	Go at your own pace Email correspondence so build a rapport Only see positive matches – no feeling of rejection

So, based on the exercise above, our proposition concept could be:

'Online dating is a proactive way of meeting people in the comfort and safety of your own home, whilst eliminating the fear of rejection.'

2. Establishing your Proposition Edge

A proposition edge explains why you are better at delivering the proposition concept than your competitors. The proposition edge is relevant when the proposition concept doesn't need to be explained.

For example, a hairdresser wouldn't need to sell the concept of 'cutting people's hair when it gets too long.'

A plumber doesn't need to sell the concept of 'repairing leaky pipes'. Airlines don't need to sell the benefits of 'flying'. Hairdressers, plumbers and airlines do, however, need to differentiate their firms from their competitors.

A good example of how the proposition concept/edge dynamic works is in the mobile phone sector. We all know what a mobile phone does and most of us recognise that we need one. It's hard to imagine now but in the early '90s the mobile phone industry had to convince us of the proposition concept. People just didn't see why we needed them.

Now that the product has matured, networks now spend their energies on differentiating their product from their competitors (i.e. the proposition edge) by offering bundle packages and hardware incentives.

But getting back to *Love Finder*. We have established the concept but, unfortunately, we are not the only internet dating organisation in the marketplace. We therefore need to think about how our proposition differentiates ourselves from our competitors, i.e. what is the proposition edge?

To establish our proposition edge we need to define:

- Our key competitors (by name or by type)

- Why we are better

Who else does our concept?	Why should they choose us instead?
Large sites (e.g. Dating Direct/ Match.com)	We are cheaper We save time by selecting a hot list We assign a personal account manager
Smaller sites	Our brand – we use A-list celebrities Our website is user-friendly We offer a money-back guarantee
Sites that promote adult services	Our moral code is guaranteed All details posted on site are vetted Privacy is protected

We are now in a position where we can differentiate our proposition from our competitors based on the brainstorm above, depending on who we are selling against.

If you don't have any competition, you don't need to explain your proposition edge. The chances are, though, if your proposition concept is a good one, it won't be long before someone else wants a piece of the marketplace.

60 Second Summary:
Define Value Proposition

Belief

Attitude doesn't set altitude. Altitude comes from a genuine belief in your Value Proposition. Belief in your value proposition is created by using 'doublethink', i.e. why someone would buy from you, and why they wouldn't.

Creating a Value Proposition

A value proposition should be simple (i.e. no marketing speak) and clearly explain how it meets the solution match, i.e. compelling need + credible solution.

Proposition Concept/Edge

Depending on the maturity of the product/service, value propositions are created by defining either the Proposition Concept, or the Proposition Edge:

i) Proposition Concept

For a relatively immature product/service, the proposition concept needs to be established.

You need to explain what it does, how it meets the prospect's needs and why your way is better than any other method.

ii) Proposition Edge

For a mature product/service the proposition edge needs to be established. You need to identify the key competitors (by name or by type) and why you are better than they are.

Worksheet: Define Value Proposition

1. Value Proposition

Our customers' most likely compelling need is:

_____

Our credible solution to meet this need is:

_____

Our credible solution is different because:

_____

2. Proposition Concept

How mature is your product? Do you need to sell the concept of your product/service?
If yes, fill in the table below:

How else could the customer solve the need?	What's the problem with this way?	Why do it your way?
	▪ ▪	▪ ▪
	▪ ▪	▪ ▪
	▪ ▪	▪ ▪

3. Proposition Edge

Do other companies provide your product/service?
If yes, fill in the table below:

Who else does the concept? (name of company or types of companies)	Why should the customer choose you?
	■ ■ ■
	■ ■ ■
	■ ■ ■

Chapter Three:
Establish Credibility

Exposing Sales Myth #3:
People Buy People

"Credibility is like virginity. Once you lose it, you can never get it back."

Anon

Ronnie the Rep:

"Everyone knows people buy people. My customers love me. I'm the only reason my customers buy from our company. They are more friends than customers. If I left here they would come with me. Customers love me even when I am cold-calling. I use my charm and wit to get the receptionist on board because when you make them your friend, you're in!"

Textbook Tarquin:

"Ummm. I wish customers loved me the way that they love Ronnie. When he is on the phone to one of his customers you would think he is calling up one of his pals; they get on so well. I'm sure that's how he gets a lot of his business. We even have customers who will speak only to Ronnie, so there must be some truth in 'people buy people'. And I hate making cold calls. Prospects clearly don't want to talk to salespeople and I feel like I am bothering them. It's tough picking yourself up when you get so much rejection."

The Single Principled Salesperson:

"People buy from me only when my product cost-effectively meets their needs. No amount of schmoozing with a client will make up for a poor product match. Every call I make (whether it be a phone call or meeting) is warm in some way, not cold. I prepare my value proposition and credibility statement for that customer in advance. I want to be in the position that, when a prospect takes my call, it will be different from all the other sales calls they receive that day."

Gift of the Gab

My father was a great salesman, a Single Principled Salesperson. When I was a boy I always leapt at the chance to visit his sales office in the school holidays. The sales office in those pre-PC and laptop days was a pretty primitive environment. The salesman, and they did all seem to be men, had a desk, a chair, and a phone. The sales manager had a bigger desk, a bigger chair and two phones. I never did ask why they had two phones. On the wall was a target board with each salesperson's name, under which lay a space where they would write their sales figures for that day/week.

My father would introduce me to the team, and then go off to fill in the board with a number that was always more than the other guys below him. His colleagues would all come up to me and tell me how proud I should be of my father. "He's got the gift of the gab; a natural born salesman," they would all say.

So I learnt from an early age that my father was a sales god; a legend. As I sat in the corner of the office pretending to do my homework, I also discovered that selling, or so I thought at the time, was all about the art of charm, persuasion and guile. They were gladiators in the sales arena; larger-than-life characters that simply oozed charisma. They traded stories of how they stalked and captured their prey. The verbal banter flew around the office, interrupted only by the occasional "pardon my French" directed towards me as they apologised for swearing. Their passion hooked me in. That was it. I wanted to be a salesman.

Yes-But, No-But

One of my first sales jobs after finishing my degree was with a replacement window company. As a young double-glazing salesman I would boldly walk into the prospect's house, window samples tucked under my arm. Based on what I'd learnt as a kid, I went on the charm offensive. I spent the first half an hour patting the prospect's dog, having a laugh with their kids, praising their house and admiring the video collection. By the time I'd finished I was being invited to their daughter's wedding reception!

The thing was it didn't take long to realise that there was no correlation between my success rate and how much they liked me. Some of my biggest sales were with grumpy folk who had no time for chit-chat. Some of my biggest wastes of time were the really, really nice people who spent the whole evening telling me how much they loved me and my windows. Always to be followed up with a "we just need to speak to the bank/brother-in-law/dog before we can make a decision." I called them the 'yes, buts'.

Every day thereafter they would apologise for not having made a decision yet. The fact was they were never going to make a decision. Lesson learnt. They were not buying me. They were buying my product. And I hadn't convinced them to buy it.

The Over-Friendly Cold-Caller

I get very frustrated when salespeople call me up and try to be my best friend. Do you get as angry as I do when cold-called by the over-friendly telesales agent? The first question they ask is "How are you today?"

What are they expecting me to say? "I was feeling a little lonely and in need of some company but now you've called I can rejoice. Let's chat for a while."? No, at best they get the curt "Fine, thank you". At worst, "I was good until you interrupted me, now go away".

I would rather they had a credible reason for their call than pretend to be my friend.

Here's the point:

People don't buy people. People buy credibility.

No amount of charm was going to get someone to buy my windows if they didn't find the product solution credible. Sure, they were polite in their rejection because they liked me, but it was still a 'no' all the same.

Being personable is, of course, important in sales. But isn't it important in all vocations? Friendly plumbers are more pleasant to deal with than unfriendly plumbers. Friendly bus-drivers are more pleasant to deal with than unfriendly bus-drivers. Friendly lawyers are more pleasant to deal with than unfriendly lawyers (unless they're on your team of course!).

Ken Hubbard, the American writer, said "Beauty is only skin deep, but it's a valuable asset if you're poor or haven't any common sense!"

In the good old/bad old days, salespeople would use their charm (a salesperson's equivalent of 'beauty') to cover up for this lack of a credible solution (a salesperson's 'common sense'). Today's professional buyer can see through that. It's what is underneath all the 'hot air' that counts most.

Cold-Calling

"There is no such thing as 'soft sell' and 'hard sell.' There is only 'smart sell' and 'stupid sell'"

Charles Browder (author)

When you first make contact with a prospect it is vital that you engage them by establishing your credibility and demonstrating that there will be something in the conversation for them.

No-one likes making cold calls. Cold-calling is hard work. Pounding the phone looking for a needle in a haystack is laborious if you are achieving little success. It's the tough end of selling where prospects don't want to talk to you and every call blends into one. Ronald Reagan, the former American President, said, "It's true hard work never killed anybody, but I figure, why take the chance?"

But it doesn't have to be like that. In fact, it should never be like that.

We recently worked with a call centre which had implemented automated dialling. Telesales agents sat in their 'chicken coops', waiting for a beep in their headsets which indicated that someone had answered the phone. Prior to automated dialling, the agents were speaking to 4 people per hour, if they were lucky. With automated dialling it became 20 people per hour.

Despite an increase in call volumes, however, the level of sales did not increase at the same rate. Indeed, making more calls per hour actually reduced their ability to sell as they became even more robotic and un-enthused than ever before. We threw away their scripts and helped the agents to actually engage with the prospect by having a credible conversation. Unsurprisingly, sales soon mirrored the increase in call volumes.

Here's why:

The secret to making cold calls is to turn them into warm calls.

Credibility Statements

Cold calls are turned into warm calls by delivering a Credibility Statement. I examine two types of credibility statements in this chapter:

A) At the start of a cold call

B) At the start of a meeting

A) Credibility Statements at the Start of a Cold Call

A credibility statement is made up of the following key elements:

1) 'Knowing' the Customer

2) Having a good 'Reason to Call'

3) 'Delivering your Credentials'

4) Demonstrating a '30 Second Case Study Value Proposition'

5) Applying the '3 Phrase Rule' and using a 'Conversation Opener'

1) Knowing the Customer

Ask for the person by their first and last name. This may sound obvious but the second you get their name wrong, or call them by Mr/Mrs it is obvious you are making a cold call.

There really is no excuse for not knowing the person's name in this age of information technology. There are good quality data companies out there who will provide the details of the buyer. As these are not always 100% accurate it is a good idea to verify with the receptionist (if applicable) that you have the correct details.

2) Reason for the Call

You need to differentiate your call from all the other calls they will receive today, i.e. why are you calling?

If your answer is, "To introduce my company" or, "To tell them about our products and services" then, I'm sorry to inform you that you are making a cold call! And you sound just like everyone else.

Often these phone calls go a little like this:

"Hi. My name is X from Y company. The reason for my call is to introduce our company to you and see if we can help you. Do you have 5 minutes?"

This all sounds professional enough, but my guess is that they will not give you 5 minutes because you haven't *earned the right* to speak with them. The prospect gets phone calls like this all the time, and they will be on autopilot in their reply of "No thanks, we are not interested."

After you have had a few responses like this your heart starts to sink and your head drops. Your cold-calling session becomes a struggle, and it turns into a numbers game. Sure, if you make enough calls you'll find someone who is interested, eventually. But it's a lot of hard work for little gain.

There is a better way.

Mark Blackmore

Imagine how positive you would feel picking up the phone if the reason you were calling was for one of the following reasons:

- "I was referred by x"
- "I met your colleague and he suggested I call"
- "I am aware that you have just launched x initiative"
- "We work with one of your main competitors x…"
- "I am aware of the specific issue you have right now, and we have helped company x with the same problem"

Your chances of earning the right to some more time with the customer will go up dramatically when you differentiate yourself by delivering a really powerful 'Reason for the Call.'

The following are excellent Reasons for the Call:

a) Referrals

Probably the most neglected tool used by salespeople is the referral.

I remember working with a telecommunications company and we implemented a referral drive whereby the sales team were rewarded with a lead for every referral obtained. They didn't like it. It was all too 'insurance salesman' for them and a big inconvenience. The team, however, reluctantly went along with the incentive. A year later we reviewed all the orders from the previous year. 80% of the largest orders were not from sales leads, as they had all assumed, but were in fact from referrals.

Why? Choosing a new supplier is always a risky decision, and a recommendation from a third party means your foot is well and truly in the client's door before you even utter a word.

Analyse your own new orders over the last 12 months. It is unlikely that the majority of the largest deals would have come from a cold source. Normally, they had heard of you from somewhere else.

The insurance industry understands the value of referrals. So why doesn't everyone else ask for referrals?

My father used to have a cartoon in his office of a bloke sitting on the loo, with the caption below saying "the job isn't finished until the paperwork is done!" Well, I'd like to revise that. It should read, "The sales call isn't finished until you've asked for a referral."

So how do you go about getting referrals? Well, it's simply a case of just asking everyone. Start off with your existing clients. Make it part of your sale to end with the sentence:

"Just before I go, is there anyone else who you think would be interested in our product/service?"

Don't be disheartened if you get a "no." People genuinely go blank at this question. This is why most salespeople who have asked for referrals quickly give up as they think it doesn't work.

To increase your chances you need to give customers a prompt to point them in the right direction. Ask who else works in their building, or next door. Or ask if they know anyone else in their position/sector.

But what if you're making a cold call and you haven't been referred? Can you still use the referral credibility statement? Yes! The key is to simply try contacting people in other parts of the organisation before making your pitch to the decision-maker.

For example, imagine you wanted to speak to the buyer of a manufacturing company employing 1000 people. You want to sell them a new product that will reduce their production time. Rather than go directly to the buyer you would be wise to contact the factory first, gaining information about the issues they are facing. With this information you have a great way of introducing yourself to the buyer, explaining that you understand their problems. In the worst case, the factory workers will just *refer* you to the buying department as they don't get involved in purchasing. There, you have it. A referral! Now when you call the buyer you can tell them that x from the y department asked you to give them a call. You have just delivered a credible statement with very little effort.

b) Sector Issues

Most companies in a specific sector have similar issues. In the 'Define Value Proposition' phase of the DECIDE® sales process you would have identified your value proposition to meet those issues.

Another excellent Reason for the Call is to explain how you have helped other organisations with issues similar to theirs.

For example, "The reason I am calling is that, if you are like other logistics companies we deal with, you are probably finding margins are getting squeezed right now. Is that right?"

"Well, we have helped a number of logistics companies increase their margins by x%"

The greater the need, the more chance you have of buying some time with the customer.

c) Company Initiatives

Company initiatives (both their company and yours) are good Reasons for the Call. Their company initiatives show them that you know something about their business. Try to gain credibility by knowing something more than could be gleaned from reading their website. Can you find out any press release information on *Lexus Nexus* or *Google*, for example?

Your company initiatives are less powerful, unless it is something that you are absolutely sure the customer will want to hear more about. Be honest with yourself though. Is the initiative compelling enough to walk you through the door?

3) Delivering your Credentials

What credibility does you or your company have? Should I respect your opinion?

It is important to be personally credible when engaging a customer and trying to gain their trust. Your credentials are made up of your personal and corporate qualifications, experience, client list and unique selling points.

a) Qualifications

Qualifications and accreditations give you credibility because they are third-party endorsed. You're not saying how fabulous you are; the badge is saying it for you.

People in the legal and medical professions demonstrate their credibility by putting their qualifications after their name on business cards/emails/marketing literature. I often wonder whether the sales profession would gain more credibility in the UK if we had a nationally recognised qualification. The flip side of that is, of course, that passing an exam doesn't make you a Single Principled Salesperson.

I guess the ultimate third party endorsement is 'by Royal Appointment.' If it is good enough for the Queen, it should be good enough for the client! A colleague of mine is often hired by Buckingham Palace to teach the staff skills in management. As you can imagine, he is never shy of telling you about his work in the Royal Household!

b) Experience

Ever been accompanied by your manager on a sales call? Once the client realises your colleague is your manager they inevitably start directing their questions to them. This is because they assume that your manager will know more than you (and can agree a greater discount!).

Make sure you 'big-up' your length of service spent in the industry/organisation, not forgetting to name-drop other big companies on your CV. People get nervous when they are being handled by the new kid on the block. Knowing that somebody senior is dealing with the account gives reassurance that things will be dealt with competently. If you are inexperienced, talk about the extensive training you have received.

c) Client list

Clients with whom you are working are another great way of building credibility. The best clients to name-drop are those well-respected in their industry sector, demonstrating an understanding of their business. Name-dropping blue-chip or household names that you work with will also give kudos, i.e. if *they* deal with you, you must be good.

Warning! Beware of making too big a deal out of the fact that you work with one of their competitors. The advantage of your industry knowledge may be outweighed by the disadvantage of sensitive information potentially being disclosed.

d) 'Ests'

You may be familiar with the concept of the 'Unique Selling Point'. This is something that is unique to you and differentiates you from your competitors.

We call USPs **'ests'.** This is because the adjective normally ends in 'est': e.g. largest, biggest, fastest, newest, oldest, smallest, coldest, hottest, smoothest, etc. An 'est' sets you apart from your competition and, if used effectively, is an excellent way of establishing credibility.

What 'ests' do you have? If you have it, flaunt it!

4) 30 Second Case Study Value Proposition

In step 1 of the DECIDE® sales process I discussed the importance of defining the value proposition. The '30 Second Case Study Value Proposition' is a snappy, yet powerful, summary of the proposition, using an example of who has benefitted from your intervention.

It is structured as follows:

"When working with 'x' company/sector *(case study)*, we found that 'y' was a real concern for them *(compelling need)*, which we solved by 'z' *(credible solution)*.

5) The 3 Phrase Rule and Conversation Opener

a) 3 Phrase Rule

The '3 Phrase Rule' is incredibly valuable when making a telephone call to a prospect.

Ever had those annoying calls from a call centre where the salesperson is reading the words from a script? You are not invited to speak until they have got through their spiel and when they eventually finish you either put the phone down or tell them you are not interested.

The 3 Phrase Rule prevents your well-planned credibility statement sounding like a script. Here it is:

Never deliver more than three phrases at the start of a cold sales call without asking a question.

Ignoring the 3-Phrase Rule would sound like this:

"Hi Mr X. It's Mark Blackmore here from Toffee Heaven. The reason for my call is Joan Smith in your Ingredients Division suggested I contact you regarding our new caramel ingredient.

We supply Masterfoods and Cadburys and Joan thought that you would be interested because it is cheaper than your current ingredient and is more consistent in quality. Latest research in y has proven that it is 14% thicker than its nearest rival and 10% lower in cost...."

 What is wrong with this?

The ingredients (sorry for the pun) of the pitch are all good, i.e. the referral from Joan; the compelling need of the customer; the credibility statement; the killer stats. But it is all too much and sounds like a sales robot is making the call.

The pitch needs to be turned into a conversation by asking a 'Conversation Opener.'

b) The Conversation Opener

To deliver the '3 Phrase Rule' we need to ask a question (i.e. the Conversation Opener) within 3 phrases.

The example above therefore would look like this:

"Hi Mr X. It's Mark Blackmore here from Toffee Heaven (phrase 1). The reason for my call is I've been speaking to Joan Smith in your Ingredients Division (phrase 2) and she suggested I gave you a call regarding our new caramel ingredient (phrase 3)."

Conversation Opener: "I believe from Joan you are the person who deals with caramel buying, is that right?"

"We supply Masterfoods and Cadburys (phrase 1) and Joan thought that you would be interested in speaking with me (phrase 2) because it is cheaper than your current ingredient and is more consistent in quality" (phrase 3).

Conversation Opener: "I believe that both of those areas are important to you?"

"Latest research has proven that it is 14% thicker than its nearest rival and 10% lower in cost...etc.

The conversation openers have turned the script into a conversation. Good conversation openers simply ask a question based on what was previously said.

Bad conversation openers include:

"How are you?" (Unless you know them)

"Do you have time to talk?" (Normally this will be greeted with a "no" unless you have delivered a powerful credibility statement)

"Have you heard of us?" (If they say no you are already on the back foot)

"Isn't it a nice day today?" (Who cares?!)

Gatekeepers

A frequently-asked question on our sales training programmes at Lammore is "How do I deal with gatekeepers?" Have you ever been flummoxed by the gatekeeper's classic line of attack, "Does he/she know you?"

There is so much drivel written about gatekeepers from 'Make them your Best Friend' to 'Show them who's Boss.'

The 'Make them your Best Friend' tactic doesn't work because it relies on the 'people buy people' sales myth. The reality is that a good P.A. will only put you through if they believe their boss would want to speak to you.

The 'Show them who's Boss' technique doesn't work because it depends on bullying your way through the door.

When they ask "Who's Calling?" you reply with first name only and sound abrupt as if 'time is money'. In my experience replying with "John" normally begs the question "John Who?"!

By far the most powerful way of getting through a gatekeeper is to create a really strong Reason for the Call.

If it is good enough to earn the right to speak with the decision-maker, I guarantee it will be good enough to get through the gatekeeper.

B) Credibility Statements at the Start of a Meeting

At the start of a meeting it is also important to deliver a strong Credibility Statement.

It will run along the same lines as for a telephone prospect call, but with a couple of additions: 'Confirm the Agenda' and 'The Bridging Question'.

1) Knowing the Customer – it is assumed at this point you do know them
2) Reason to Call – it is still worth reiterating why you are there
3) Delivering your Credentials – remind them of your credibility
4) 30 Second Case Study Value Proposition – less important as you will go into more depth during the meeting
5) Confirm the Agenda – the purpose of stating the agenda is to tell them the format proposed for the meeting. This will be:

    i) You are going to ask them some questions about their business (i.e. identify compelling need)

    ii) You are then going to tell them about your business (i.e. deliver credible solution)

    iii) Together you can then agree next steps (i.e. ensure perceived value)

6) 3 Phrase Rule and Conversation Opener – less valid as they will listen more openly than on a cold call.

7) The Bridging Question – this is the question that gets you into the 'Confirm Opportunity' part of the DECIDE® Sales Process.

60 Second Summary:
Establish Credibility

People don't buy people. People buy credibility.

The secret to making *cold calls* is to turn them into *warm calls.*

Credibility Statements at the Start of a Cold Call

A Credibility Statement when cold calling is made up of the following key elements:

1) Knowing the Customer
- Ensure you know the person's first and second names

2) Having a good Reason to Call
- Referrals
- Sector issues
- Company initiatives

3) Delivering your Credentials
- Qualifications
- Experience
- Client List
- 'Ests'

4) Demonstrating a 30 Second Case Study Value Proposition
- Case Study + Compelling Need + Credible Solution

5) Applying the 3 Phrase Rule and using a Conversation Opener
Never say more than 3 phrases without asking the prospect a question

The Gatekeeper
The most effective way of getting through a gatekeeper is to create a strong Reason for the Call.

Credibility Statement at the Start of Meeting
As above, but add 'Confirm the Agenda' and 'The Bridging Question.'

Worksheet: Establish Credibility

Credibility Statements at the Start of a Cold Call
Choose a buyer you are trying to make an appointment with:

a) Know the Customer
Name

_____

Position

_____

b) Reason for Call
"The reason for my call is....

_____
_____
_____
_____
_____

How compelling is it? Does it sound like you know something about them, or does it sound like another cold call?

c) Deliver your Credentials
Qualifications; Experience; Client List; 'Ests'

_____
_____
_____
_____
_____

d) 30 Second Case Study Value Proposition
Case Study + Compelling Need + Credible Solution

_____

_____

_____

_____

_____

e) Conversation Openers
List some of the conversation openers that you may wish to use

_____

_____

_____

_____

_____

Chapter Four:
Confirm Opportunity

Exposing Sales Myth #4:
Customers Like to Talk about
Themselves

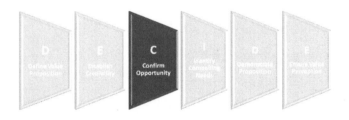

"You don't want a million answers as much as you want a few forever 'questions'. The questions are diamonds you hold in the light. Study a lifetime and you see different colors from the same jewel."
   Richard Bach (author of Jonathan Livingston Seagull)

Mark Blackmore

Ronnie the Rep:

"Customers appreciate you showing an interest in them, and everyone loves talking about themselves.

So I never talk business. I talk about their favourite football teams, the names of their kids, their favourite pint, where they went on their holidays. They love the opportunity and will chat away forever."

Textbook Tarquin:

"Customers appreciate it if you ask them questions about their business. So I find out everything there is to know about the customer: the company; their role; their products; the decision-making process; their suppliers; their history; their mission statement; their corporate values. I have been known to spend 2 hours with a customer asking questions about their business in the past. I walk away from meetings with my pad full of information and happy I have done a good job. Meanwhile my prospect feels good about the fact that they have finally seen a salesperson who listens."

The Single Principled Salesperson:

"Sure, you have to ask questions...but they need to be the right questions. Why should a customer spend their valuable time telling you information they already know? There is a certain amount of information I need to identify in a meeting, such as the size of the opportunity and the decision-making process. But I appreciate that this is for my benefit, not theirs. I keep these questions to an absolute minimum or, better still, find out as much as I can prior to meeting the client."

The Good, the Bad and the Ugly

Here's a quick survey. How much time do you spend in your current sales calls on the following areas of the sales process?:

- Identifying Compelling Needs and Confirming Opportunity (e.g. questioning): ____%

- Demonstrating Proposition (e.g. pitching): ___%

- Ensuring Perceived Value (e.g. closing/negotiating): ___%

If you are spending less than 50% of your time 'Confirming Opportunity' and 'Identifying Compelling Needs' you are spending too much time 'selling' and not enough time 'consulting.' In doing so you are self-focused, and not customer-focused. This is not the way of the Single Principled Salesperson .But then many of you know that I'm sure. So here is a follow-up survey.

Look at the time you spend on questioning. What is the split between 'Identifying Compelling Needs' (questions which identify their problems and desires) and 'Confirming Opportunity' (questions which identify factual information about the customer and the size of the opportunity)?:

- Identifying Compelling Needs ___%

- Confirming Opportunity ___%

The result of this survey is important. If you are spending less than half of your time 'Identifying Compelling Needs' you are missing the real reason for questioning. Let me explain.

I have sat in on thousands of sales calls. Some were good. Some were bad. And some were downright ugly. The bad ones were those where the salesperson didn't ask any questions at all. They launched in with their features and benefits without any consideration for what the buyer may actually need. It's like watching an old war film where the soldier sprays bullets randomly, hoping that some will hit their target. And of course some do, which is why these salespeople, no matter how bad, will get a sale, eventually.

Then there were the ugly calls, mainly because I was so embarrassed to be there. The salesperson knew that they had to conduct a fact find and gain as much information about the customer as possible. So they launched into a 'Spanish Inquisition', asking a list of meaningless questions that do nothing but bore the customer.

I remember one very conscientious salesperson who, eager to impress, asked a whole series of questions. We were selling advertising and I remember standing in a car repair garage underneath a railway arch in Peckham, London.

The owner of the garage was a genuine prospect and was obviously interested in placing an ad. It all started well enough until the interrogation began. He began by discussing the MOT side of the business: How long had they been established as an MOT centre? How many of their mechanics were qualified in conducting MOTs? What was special about their MOT service? How did they advertise their MOTs? What was their turnover on MOTs? What was their profit on MOTS? Who were their competitors on MOTs? How much did they charge for MOTs? And so it went on, and on, and on. Once he finished asking about MOTs he then went on to ask the same set of questions regarding the *servicing* part of the business! The poor customer kept looking over to me to see if I could somehow put an end to it all. Mercy killings for buyers: now there's a good product opportunity!

The salesperson was just doing his job, or so he thought. He had been trained to say all of this on the induction course, so I guess it really wasn't his fault. The problem was that at the end of a painfully boring hour, we had gathered lots of information about the customer but we hadn't established any *needs*. And needs make sales; not information. If we were writing an article entitled 'A day in the life of a Peckham Car Mechanic', it would have been a wonderful use of everyone's time. But we were not. We were supposed to be selling him an advert.

Here's the point:

Customers want to talk about their needs and how you can help them; not about themselves.

Confirming the Opportunity: IQ Questions

So are all questions about the customer's circumstances irrelevant? No. There is a certain amount of *information* that needs to be discovered to be able to present a proposal. This will include finding out about the customer's current situation and the decision-making process (i.e. Information Questions). The salesperson also needs to *qualify* the size of the opportunity and establish its potential (i.e. Qualification Questions).

These questions are collectively called **'IQ Questions'** ('IQ' = Information/Qualification). Without them it is difficult to make a recommendation and know whether the opportunity is worth fighting for.

Watch the predators in the nightclub and admire their ability to gain information and qualify their prey by asking IQ Questions:

"What do you do for a living?" (Stockbroker: good answer; Shop Assistant: bad answer)

"What car do you drive?" (Ferrari: good answer; I take the bus: bad answer)

"Where do you live?" (Chelsea: good answer; With my mum: bad answer)

"Are you single?" (Yes: good answer; No: irrelevant depending on the answers above!)

What information do *you* need when selling your products or services?

In *advertising* we used the acronym 'WHATS' to gain the information:

- *W*hat is the business?
- *H*ow do they currently get their enquiries?
- *A*rea: Where do they want to attract people from?
- *T*arget market: What type of customer do they want?
- *S*pecial features: What differentiates them from their competitors?

For *payroll services* you could ask:

- Is the payroll currently outsourced or handled in-house?
- If in-house, how many staff are employed in the accounts team?
- How many payslips are processed per month?
- How frequently is the payroll run?
- What software is used to run the payroll?
- Who makes the decisions re payroll?

    Estate agents would want to establish from a potential buyer:

- What is their current situation? (e.g. first time buyer/something to sell/investment property)
- How are they planning on buying the property? (e.g. mortgage/cash)
- What is their budget?
- What is on their criteria list? (e.g. number of bedrooms; location; garden, etc)

Armed with this information the salesperson in the advertising company/payroll bureau/estate agency would be able to make a recommendation.

A glance at any Customer Relationship Management (CRM) system will tell you the type of information that could (and in some cases should) be obtained. This will include: account information; decision-maker details and process; type of business; current supplier; type of products/service used; quantity & price of current goods; bank details; previous history, etc.

The problem with many salespeople is that IQ Questions are the only questions they ask, and they ask too many of them. The result is that they bore the customer and often end up just pitching like-for-like against the incumbent supplier.

Nowhere is this more prevalent than in a commodity sales environment. The 'stack 'em high'- sell 'em cheap' mentality reduces the sales process to finding out what the customer is currently using and offering a cheaper alternative. In these cases the company may as well just email a price list to the customer and cut out the middle man, i.e. the salesperson.

This approach makes it impossible to sell premium brands and, other than saving the customer some money, the salesperson never adds any real value or builds any loyalty.

The Single Principled Salesperson, however, identifies what the customer *needs*, not simply what they *have*. In doing so they ensure that they fully deliver a solution that truly adds value.

This can only be done by moving quickly on from asking IQ Questions to questions that 'Identify Compelling Needs', which is covered in the next chapter.

60 Second Summary:
Confirm Opportunity

IQ Questions

'IQ Questions' (i.e. Information/Qualification Questions) identify information about the customer and qualify the size/nature of the opportunity.

IQ Questions are important to the salesperson in deciding whether the account has potential. They add, however, no value to the client and do not identify reasons to buy.

Too many IQ questions will turn the buyer off. Customers want to talk about their compelling needs.

Worksheet: Confirm Opportunity

IQ Questions

What information do you need to identify from the customer?

List the information and qualification criteria you require from the customer:

Information & Qualification Criteria

Chapter Five:
Identify Compelling Needs

Exposing Sales Myth #5:
It's a Numbers Game

"The secret of success is learning how to use pain and pleasure"

Anthony Robins

Ronnie the Rep:

"My sales manager keeps going on about creating a pipeline. Pipeline *schmipeline!* I don't need to record pitches on a fancy spreadsheet to know whether I'm going to hit target. I'm a big game hunter. I have an affinity for sniffing out the big deals. One deal and I hit my target. I admit that if it doesn't come in I miss, but then that's selling. That's Ronnie."

Textbook Tarquin:

"It's definitely a numbers game. My pipeline is the size of an Alaskan oil feed! I am aware, of course, that they won't all close. So I apply the scientific formula assigned by the CRM system. Currently, the pessimistic forecast is that I am going to double my target, whilst the optimistic target is that I should be able to retire after this month, although I must admit that it never seems to work out that way! Because even when I think they should close, they don't. Why is that?"

The Single Principled Salesperson:

"For once I agree with Ronnie...kind of! When it comes to forecasting, it really isn't a numbers game. Having a whole heap of deals on an Excel spreadsheet can give you the impression that all is rosy in the garden. Except a large percentage of those deals will never materialise. This is not because the customer chose someone else. They just didn't choose anyone. The key to forecasting is assessing the extent to which the customer has to take action. Ask yourself the question, "What would happen if they did nothing?" The bigger the consequence or benefit of taking action, the greater will be the customer's necessity to do something."

Needs make Sales

In the previous chapter I proposed that the mistake too many salespeople make when selling is they ask lots of the wrong *type* of questions. They gather lots of meaningless information which adds nothing to the sales process. Needs make sales, not information.

But even when salespeople identify needs, they can still struggle to close the deal. Many sales managers have been duped by the 'phantom forecast,' an over-optimistic sales projection based on a pipeline of proposals that never convert into actual business. CRM systems try to improve the accuracy of forecasts by building in a %age close prediction, but still the result is often much lower than the promise.

This is because the needs identified in the sales call were not *compelling* needs. Just having a need doesn't mean that the customer will act upon it. Many of the deals in a salesperson's pipeline remain unclosed because the customer keeps procrastinating on the decision. Playing the numbers game doesn't help them deliver more sales. It just creates more work for themselves and everyone around them. It can take a whole army of people to write a proposal and if the hours were added up preparing meaningless quotations salespeople would think twice about doing them. I wince when I look back at the unproductive time I spent at weekends sending proposals to clients, most of which never closed.

The Single Principled Salesperson ensures that the needs are compelling prior to presenting the solution. Why? Because only then are they assured that the customer will be motivated into action.

Think about the decisions you make at home. What compelled you to buy that new house? You'd been thinking about it for a while but now the baby is on the way it's time for action. What compelled you to buy that new car? You'd been thinking about it for a while but now the garage has quoted on repairing the old one and it's time to get that car loan. What compelled you to buy that new sofa? You'd been thinking about it for a while but now the in-laws are coming for Xmas.

Here's the point:

Needs make sales, but only if they are compelling needs.

Imagine I walked into your local pub this evening and offered everyone the chance to double their salary. How many would be interested? If you drink in the same places I do, I'd have to beat them off with a stick! Few people are financially independent and most need to earn additional income. So they have a need, but is it a *compelling* need?

Well, it depends on how badly they need to double their salary and what they are prepared to do to get it. If my solution was to offer a job of driving a minicab between 7pm and 7am for a month whilst still doing the day job, how many people in the pub would still be interested? Not many.

Despite having the need/want/desire to double their salary, most would not be prepared to do what it takes. Their need is *passive*, not *compelling*.

Single Principled Salespeople test just how important the need is to the buyer. For example, imagine we are in the pub again and this time I ask *why* they would like to double their salary and what would be the consequence if they didn't double it. Their answers would give me a greater indication of the possibility of my offer being accepted. For example, if someone replied, "I need the money because I've just been presented with a bailiff order and if I don't pay in the next 4 weeks I lose my home", I would feel confident they would take the job. Or if they said, "I have a sick child who needs a private operation", they also have a compelling reason for listening to my offer.

If they said, however, "Well, it would be *nice* to earn a bit more", I would assume their need is *passive*, and not *compelling*. The chance of their agreeing to my proposal is severely diminished.

Single Principled Salespeople recognise this and test the buyer's commitment to taking action. The best way to identify how to turn a passive need into a compelling need is to challenge the individual's reasons for solving the need.

The IT sector was a great sector to be working in during 1999. Common belief was that on the stroke of midnight on 31st December 1999 the world's computer systems would cease to work, with aeroplanes falling out of the sky and hospital mainframes in total meltdown. To pre-empt this event the IT industry made a lot of money upgrading systems to be compatible with the 21st Century. It was a wonderful time to be in IT sales because the 'millennium bug' had created its own compelling event. Companies could not put off investing in their IT infrastructure any longer. They just had to do something. They had a compelling need.

Unfortunately, millennium bugs are not an everyday occurrence. The role of a salesperson is to create a compelling need without the threat of a global meltdown!

Pain/Gain

Needs are established by identifying a customer's desire to either achieve *gain* or to avoid/reduce *pain*.

Examples:

a) Buying a house

- *Gain*: extra bedroom; double garage; better school
- *Pain*: noisy neighbour; reduce mortgage; reduce commuting time

b) Outsource Payroll services

- *Gain*: expertise; improve reporting; improve speed of processing
- *Pain*: reduce costs; tax legislation

c) Advertising

- *Gain*: more enquiries; get company name known in marketplace; increase profit
- *Pain*: prevent bankruptcy; suppress competition

But getting the need is only half of the story. Single Principled Salespeople go one step further by ensuring the need is a *compelling* need and not just a *passive* need.

A Passive Need is something that I would like to solve or achieve, but it may not be important enough to act upon. A Compelling Need motivates a customer towards action. There are lots of sales books telling you how to identify needs. They don't tell you, however, how to create *compelling* needs.

Compelling Need Questions

To identify the motivation to move away from *pain* the sales person could ask:

"What would be the consequences of not delivering a solution to x?"

"What are the implications of not solving y?"

To identify the motivation to move towards *gain* the salesperson could ask:

"What would be the benefit of solving x?"

"How important is it that you achieve y?"

Examples of Compelling Need questions:

a) Selling a house:

"What would be the consequence of not being close to the town centre?" (Pain)

"If you couldn't find 5 bedrooms, how would that affect you?" (Pain)

"How important is it to you that you move by Christmas?" (Gain)

"What if you didn't have a garden?" (Pain)

"What if you couldn't find a house by x date?" (Pain)

b) Selling payroll services:

"What would happen if you didn't save the company £x?" (Pain)

"How would it benefit you if you could run certain reports?" (Gain)

"What are the benefits of paying your staff more quickly?" (Gain)

"What are the implications of not reducing the amount of time spent on your current payroll process?" (Pain)

c) Selling advertising:

"What would happen if you didn't receive x enquiries?" (Pain)

"How would you cope if you didn't get y type of client?" (Pain)

"What would be the consequences of not increasing your turnover to x?" (Pain)

Getting Emotional

"It's been emotional"

> *Vinny Jones as 'Big Chris' in 'Lock, Stock and Two Smoking Barrels'*

So we know that people have a need to avoid pain or achieve gain. But beware! An individual may articulate one type of need, but be hiding another much more powerful motivation to buy.

What do I mean?

Do you know anyone who owns a Ferrari? If they are male, they will probably tell you that they bought it because of the brake horsepower, the resale value or the Italian craftsmanship. If it's a Porsche they will rave about the German engineering, the 0-60 speed, etc. All of these are rational reasons for buying the car.

This is not, however, the *real* reason they bought the car. We all know the real reason.... don't we?! It is because when they drive past a shop window they like to look at their own reflection! They get an instant ego extension. Their motivation for buying the car was emotional, despite their rational justification.

Here's the point:

People buy emotionally, and justify rationally.

Let's even-up the sexism and discuss ladies' love for shoes. When a woman walks past the window of a shoe shop her eyes are captivated by a stunning pair of high-heeled wonders. At this point her mind is devoid of rational thought and she just simply has to have them. Now we all know that she doesn't actually need a new pair of shoes. But this isn't going to stop her from making the purchase. She starts to rationalise in her mind why she absolutely needs them: she has no other shoes in that colour to match the outfit she occasionally wears once every leap year; if she doesn't get them today they may not have her size next week; they are in the sale and may be full price tomorrow. The driver for the purchase is emotional but, just like the Ferrari guy, the justification is rational.

Mark Blackmore

Examples of Rational and Emotional Buying Motives:

a) Buying a house

RATIONAL	EMOTIONAL
Need more space	Keeping up with the Joneses
Investment potential	Ambition
Relocation	Self-esteem/pride
Budget	Emotional connection with area
Schools in area	Fear of market conditions
Shorter commute	Postcode

b) Outsourcing a payroll system

RATIONAL	EMOTIONAL
Reduce costs	Look good to boss
Improve reporting systems	Job retention
Improve turnaround times	Recognition for driving change
Increase workforce flexibility	Less employee hassle

c) Buying advertising

RATIONAL	EMOTIONAL
New enquiries/leads	Prestige
Sales revenue	Keeping name 'out there'
Increase market share	'One up' on competitors
New product lines	Seen to be doing something

Identifying a Compelling Need You Can Solve

Finally, make sure your questions unearth a compelling need that you can *actually* solve. I once shadowed a lady who was selling CRM software. She identified some really great needs. The problem was the needs that she identified couldn't be resolved by her product. It certainly showed her competitor in a good light though!

Alanis Morrisette sang on *Ironic*, "You've got 2,000 spoons, when all you need is a knife." If you're a spoon salesperson this isn't ironic, it's just bad selling.

Single Principled Salespeople analyse how the features of their product will meet the needs of a customer. They then set about identifying those needs, because they know they have a credible solution to match them.

60 Second Summary:
Identify Compelling Needs

Pain & Gain

Customers will only buy if they have a problem that needs to be solved (i.e. avoid pain), or there is something they want to achieve (i.e. gain).

Just having a need, however, doesn't mean that the customer will act upon it. Needs make sales, but only if they are *compelling* needs.

Compelling Need Questions

Single Principled Salespeople turn Passive Needs into Compelling Needs.

A passive need is something that an individual would like to solve or achieve, but it may not be significant enough to act upon.

A compelling need motivates a customer into action. This is tested by asking questions that challenge the consequences or benefits of dealing with the need.

Rational and Emotional Buying Motives

People buy emotionally and justify rationally. They will often tell you the rational reasons, but be aware that there will be emotional motives that will influence their decision.

Worksheet: Identify Compelling Needs

1. Rational/Emotional Buying Motives

What are the rational and emotional buying motives important to your customers when buying your products?

Rational Motives	Emotional Motives

2. Creating Compelling Needs

a) List below the key emotional and rational motives identified in the previous exercise.

b) Now write a Pain and Gain question for each one (over page).

Mark Blackmore

Buying Motive	Pain Questions	Gain Questions

Chapter Six:
Demonstrate Proposition

Exposing Sales Myth #6:
Sell the Sizzle, not the Sausage

*"All that glisters is not gold; Often have you heard that
told: Many a man his life hath sold
But my outside to behold: Gilded tombs do worms enfold."*
                                                William Shakespeare

Ronnie the Rep:

"My missus woke me up in the middle of the night last week to say I was pitching in my sleep! Doesn't surprise me – I know my pitch inside out and back to front. You could see my sales presentation 10 times and it wouldn't change. Not that I stand still. Every so often I'll hear of something new and I'll add it to my sales patter. A good rep should be slick in front of a customer. I liken myself to a Shakespearian actor on a stage. The audience expect my performance to be perfect every time."

Textbook Tarquin:

"My presentations are very professional. I always show our corporate video and the full product guide on PowerPoint to every customer. I present on my laptop because it helps me to remember what comes next and I show all of the slides because I do not want the customer to miss anything. Some customers, well actually most, complain when I start to open up the laptop, but our sales manager said we had to use them, and that's good enough for me."

Single Principled Salesperson:

"My pitch is based purely on the compelling needs I have identified earlier in the sales call. I only show the customer information that is relevant to these needs. Anything else is noise as it just dilutes the message. Great salespeople engage the buyer and give them exactly what they are looking for."

When is a Benefit not a Benefit?

I love the concept of making presentations sizzle. I have to - at Lammore we run a session called *Sizzle Selling*! My issue with the myth of 'selling the sizzle' is with how salespeople think that they can bamboozle a customer with fancy presentations that are high on show but low on substance.

At first sight, 'selling the sizzle' seems to make perfect sense. The sausage sizzling away on a griddle is much more likely to sell than an uncooked sausage sitting in the fridge. But this is because the sizzle fired up your senses, bringing attention to the fact that you are hungry. The sizzle satisfied your compelling need.

Ever smelt a sizzling sausage when you have food poisoning? It would probably make you feel even worse, because this time your need isn't hunger. In fact, food is the last thing you need.

Most salespeople use features and benefits when delivering their proposition. So when is a benefit not a benefit? Answer: when the benefit doesn't meet the need of the customer.

I popped into a high street electrical store recently because I was interested in buying a digital camera. Being a technophobe I asked the sales assistant to explain what it did. By the end of his long-winded explanation of all the camera's amazing features I decided it was probably over-specified for my needs, and decided to go elsewhere. If only the salesperson had asked me a couple of questions about how I was planning on using the camera I'd have bought it. How do I know this? Because the sales assistant in the shop next door sold me the exact same camera! By asking a few questions she established my needs and then explained the benefits of why this camera was perfect for me.

To demonstrate your proposition you need to match your credible solution with the customer's compelling need. No amount of sizzle will make up for a poor solution match. Those top of the range golf clubs are fabulous, except I am left-handed and these are right-handed clubs. The sports car looks amazing but how will my wife and 3 kids fit into 2 seats? The house is gorgeous, but it is outside of the school catchment area.

Here's the point:

Compelling needs sell the sausage, not sizzle.

Only if the customer has a compelling need will they be interested in your proposition, regardless of how much sizzle you throw at the product.

But let's assume you do have a great match to the compelling need. The next question is how should you present it? Well you've got to make it sizzle of course!

Ever ordered a sizzling dish in a Thai or Chinese restaurant? All your senses become engaged. The first engagement is your sense of hearing as the doors to the kitchen open and a magnificent roar can be heard. Then, your sense of smell is teased by the wonderful aroma drifting across the restaurant. Your sense of sight marvels at the bold colours as the dish is presented in front of you. Finally, your sense of taste confirms that it's a great choice. The experience has been enhanced by the dish's ability to engage all of your senses.

Here's the point:

The key to presenting your proposition is engagement.

Death by PowerPoint

So what are the main ways of Sizzle Selling? One thing is for sure, PowerPoint isn't one of them!

PowerPoint is the biggest perpetrator of poor quality presentations. The most feared sight in the workplace is seeing that we are on slide 23 of a 325-slide PowerPoint presentation. We stare at a projector screen, and are taken through boring, hard-to-read slides by someone we can't even see because it is dark! It doesn't matter how dynamic the animation is or how fast the words fly in at acute angles, it's still dull. Worse still, it detracts you from the salesperson doing the presentation.

Martin Waller from *The Times* wrote on 18th April 2007:

"Research from the University of New South Wales suggests that we process information best in verbal or written form, but not in both simultaneously. As so often happens, it has taken the best efforts of brainy academics to prove what most of us instinctively knew. Trying to follow what someone is saying while watching the same words on a screen is the equivalent of riding a bicycle along a crowded train. It offers the appearance of making extra progress but is actually rather impractical."

I remember an incident a few years after Microsoft PowerPoint was first launched in 1988. A colleague, who was gadget-mad, had spent days preparing an introduction for a sales meeting he was running. He kept telling me that this was the best presentation he had ever written. On the day, he excitedly set up the PC and with an air of anticipation he clicked on 'slide show' and began the automatic presentation. For the next two minutes we marvelled at the Technicolor slides with phrases appearing gymnastically onto the screen. When the show finished he stood up expecting rapturous applause. Instead all he had was a confused-looking bunch of salespeople wondering when the meeting was going to begin.

Ford Motor Company banned their managers from using PowerPoint when they identified that their managers were spending 3 hours preparing a slide show presentation for a 20-minute team meeting.

Albert Mehrabian, psychology professor at the University of California, famously identified that the message owes very little to the actual words delivered. Body language, tone, pace, intonation and volume all contribute significantly to *how* the message is received. This is why two people can tell the same joke, but only one will get the laughs (as my business partner Tim constantly reminds me). If our attention is on a computer screen, we are missing the presenter's body language and, therefore, at least half of the message is lost.

This is vital in telesales as well as face-to-face sales. Ever had a call at home from a call centre? You don't need a webcam or video-phone to know that they are reading from a script. They sound robotic, un-enthused and uninterested. When we work with call centre clients the first thing we tell them to do is throw away their scripts. Unless you are a professional newsreader it is very difficult to sound genuinely engaged when you are reading from a sheet of paper.

Call centres often approach us as they feel their salespeople do not engage the customer and do not listen. This is not surprising. The poor individual is so determined to get to the bottom of the page he doesn't have time to listen! If the customer actually interacts with them during the reading of the script it is, quite frankly, annoying!

And if PowerPoint presentations were the key to making sales, how come we can sell over the phone? No, it is not the presentation that matters, it is the *presenter*. We have analysed hundreds of great public speakers, from politicians to talk-show hosts. The following applied to every one of them. Great presenters:

- Engage an audience by relating the content to them
- Are enthusiastic
- Interact with the audience
- Make the presentation conversational
- Use stories and analogies
- Use visual aids or props to help reinforce their message, not hinder it.

Buyer Types

Some research published in 2002 grouped buyers into 4 main types (see Figure 11):

- Visionaries (keen to take the lead on a new product)

- Pragmatists (happy to purchase a new product providing someone else has already tried it)

- Conservatives (want scientific/academic proof that the product will deliver on its promises)

- Laggards (reluctant to try anything new and resistant to change)

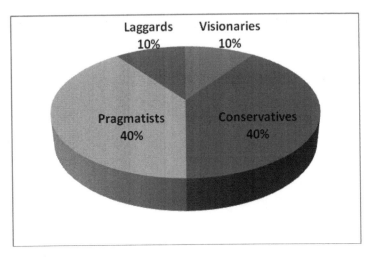

Figure 11

They identified that most buyers are either conservatives or pragmatists (80% of the buyer population). As such they feel uncomfortable being product guinea pigs. They are risk-averse, especially in large organisations or public sectors where a risky mistake could cost them their jobs. If reassured, however, they will buy new products.

As such, a Single Principled Salesperson uses Sizzle Selling techniques to prove the worth of their product.

Sizzle Selling

There are four main Sizzle Selling techniques:

- Analogies
- Case Studies
- Sketchbooks
- Killer Statistics

1. Analogies

CS Lewis, the creator of Alice in Wonderland, said, "Miracles are a retelling in small letters of the very same story which is written across the whole world in letters too large for some of us to see."

Great leaders know the power of this and help us see 'the miracles' by telling stories. Similarly, Single Principled Salespeople use analogies to move customers towards action.

I once sat down with my eldest son to try to teach him why it is important to sometimes slow down if you want to get something done quickly. Understandably he wasn't really getting it. "Less haste, more speed son", I kept reiterating. Still we were not getting anywhere. It was only then he looked up at me with an enlightened smile and said "I suppose it is a bit like the tortoise and the hare, isn't it dad?". I nodded, grinned, and reflected on how a five-year-old kid had explained my message more succinctly then any long-winded rationale I had to offer.

When selling the benefits of complicated products we urge clients to use analogies. They don't have to be children's fables like my son's, although his was a good one. They should, however, be something that the audience can relate to in everyday life.

When I worked in the IT industry I noticed most people found it difficult to explain in simple terms a technical solution. That's why most techies can't sell! They get too bogged down in the detail of the technology and lose the buyer.

We were working with a media company recently who had developed some sophisticated marketing software. I asked them to explain it to me, and within a few moments I was totally lost. Their explanation would have been OK if they were selling to software programmers, but their prospective clients were PR agencies. My experience of PR people is that they are even less interested in technology than I am. All they want to know is what sets the software apart from any other and, more importantly, how it will help their clients.

We brainstormed how we could explain the software using everyday language, and one of the delegates came up with the idea of likening it to shopping in a supermarket. The software grouped the data into aisles and, using a shopping list, selected exactly the right items to suit the customer's needs.

There were a few people in the room who had recently been through the company's induction programme. They admitted at the end of our session that this was the first time they understood what they were selling!

We hear this a lot when working with salespeople. Anxious not to look stupid, salespeople throw in buzzwords to make themselves sound impressive, yet they actually understand none of it. Like the villagers in Hans Christian Andersen's *The Emperor's New Clothes*, they do not realise that no-one else understands a word of it either.

Single Principled Salespeople understand that a naked king is of no use to anyone, so they use analogies to cover up his white bits!

The key to making analogies work for you is to use a story that makes undeniable sense in everyday life. Shopping is a useful analogy depending on your selling scenario. Imagine you sell a premium product (at a premium price) and you need to convince the buyer that it is foolish to go to a cheaper, non-specialist supplier. An analogy could be to discuss car-buying, as most people when buying a top-of-the-range Mercedes, for example, would be more likely to go to a main dealership as they offer perceived quality of service and peace of mind.

2. Case Studies

Edmund Burke, the political philosopher, said *"Example* is the school of mankind, and they will learn at no other."

I discussed Case Studies (or *examples* in Edmund Burke speak) in Chapter 3 on 'Establish Credibility', and another great storytelling tool in the Single Principled Salesperson's kitbag is the case study. Like analogies they take the customer through a journey to reinforce the message, only this time the story relates to the buyer's business. Great salespeople explain how they helped a company who had similar problems to theirs, and how they were solved. They deliver weight to your claim that you can solve the buyer's issue. People feel comforted in the knowledge that they are not alone in having their problem, and that you are experienced in solving it. Throw in the name of a client they respect and your solution becomes very credible.

3. Sketchbooks

Which brings us onto the third Sizzle Selling technique used by Single Principled Salespeople: the Sketchbook.

Pablo Picasso said "I paint objects as I think them, not as I see them." The problem with PowerPoint slides, apart from the fact they act like sedatives, is that they are already finished, i.e. you already see them. So trying to get someone involved in the journey is difficult. The sketchbook technique gets engagement because it creates involvement.

Ever built an Airfix model or completed a jigsaw? It was the journey that made it fun, not the end result. A sketchbook, like the building of a model aeroplane, takes the prospect by the hand and guides them through your solution.

Take our media company described above. The team showed me a series of slides demonstrating one of their products. It basically segmented the marketplace by profiling the client's target audience. Again, I was none the wiser after I'd seen the slide show. One of the delegates told us about his novel approach to presenting this particular product. He said that all he did was simply take a blank piece of paper, draw lots of dots, and then, depending on the client's target audience, start to split the dots into sections. He had never admitted it because he thought that maybe he was over-simplifying their award-winning software. When he finished his sketchbook presentation he received a standing ovation! Everyone agreed that the sketchbook analogy made more sense than the slide show had ever done.

So ditch your slide show, and pull out your sketchbook.

4. Killer Statistics

People love statistics. Well 93% of people do anyway. Ok, I made that up. But statistics add weight to what you are saying, despite Benjamin Disraeli, the ex British Prime Minister, saying, "There are lies, damn lies, and statistics." People want proof that your product is as good as you say it is.

Ever heard the phrase "All buyers are liars"? Well, buyers will often be heard saying "All sales tell tales!"

So being able to back up your story with a well-researched statistic is important. And that is the key. The power of the statistic is in the source. If you can't back it up, don't use it.

I spent some time in the US recently and got hooked on watching their 'infomercials', i.e. TV ads that last 15 minutes or so. If you study them closely they will ALWAYS quote a killer stat that just makes you have to buy it: the golf club that is guaranteed to add 30+ yards to your drive; the frying pan that reduces fat content by 38%; the vacuum cleaner that picks up 87% more dirt than the No. 1 brand.

When matching a compelling need, statistics can be the nudge that buyers need to make a decision, so get quoting your numbers.

60 Second Summary:
Demonstrate Proposition

Compelling needs sell the sausage, not sizzle.

Fancy presentations will not make up for a bad value proposition. Furthermore, PowerPoint should be used to demonstrate graphics, not to bombard the audience with text.
There are 4 methods of Sizzle Selling:

1. Analogies
Single Principled Salespeople are great storytellers. The key to making analogies work for you is to use a story that makes undeniable sense in everyday life.

2. Case Studies
Case Studies deliver weight to your claim that you have a track record in solving the buyer's issue. Throw in the name of a client they respect and your solution becomes very credible.

3. Sketchbooks
The problem with a PowerPoint slide is that it is already finished, so trying to get someone involved in the journey is difficult. The sketchbook technique gets engagement by simply drawing the process in front of the buyer.

4. Killer Statistics

People love statistics. When matching a compelling need, statistics can be the nudge that buyers need to reinforce in their mind that they are making the right decision.

Mark Blackmore

Worksheet: Demonstrate Proposition

1. Analogies
Which stories can you use to explain your message/solution? To help you with this, first write down the key sales point you are trying to make. Then brainstorm an everyday situation where your key sales point is obvious. Useful scenarios to choose from are: food shopping; buying cars; mobile phones; family holidays; kids; travel.

_____
_____
_____
_____

2. Case Studies
Which case studies can you use to explain your solution?

_____
_____
_____
_____

3. Sketchbook
What processes could be explained using the sketchbook technique?

_____
_____
_____
_____

4. Killer Stats
Which killer stats can you use to reinforce your product solution?

_____
_____
_____

Chapter Seven:
Ensuring Perceived Value

Exposing Sales Myth #7:
Money Talks

'Quality is remembered long after the price is forgotten'
Gucci Slogan

Ronnie the Rep:

"When it comes down to it, the customer just wants the cheapest he can get. You can talk about 'added value' until the cows come home, but they are not interested. Tell them about the bells and whistles and it just looks like you are trying to pull the wool over their eyes. 'Money talks', make no mistake. It always has, and always will. Just as well my customers like me, otherwise the way this company has put the prices up they would have walked years ago."

Textbook Tarquin:

"We recently put our prices up and you should have seen the reaction of the customers – they were livid! I explained that it wasn't my fault and I try wherever possible to ease the pain by discounting. Despite this, the customer keeps threatening to go elsewhere. One day I guess they will."

Single Principled Salesperson:

"Customers want value, not the cheapest price. If people wanted cheap we would all be driving around in 10-year-old cars and shopping in charity shops. Products are only perceived as expensive if the value is not appreciated by the customer. I have never lost a deal on price, only on value."

The Toothpaste Challenge

How much do you spend on toothpaste? Try this exercise – try to guess how much each of these toothpaste products cost in the UK? Write down your answers.

1. Asda Smart Price 50ml

Answer: _____

2. Colgate Total 50ml

Answer: _____

3. Green People Organic 50ml

Answer: _____

4. Rembrandt Plus 50ml

Answer: _____

The answers are at the end of the chapter. How close were you? If you are like most people you were pretty close in getting *Colgate* correct. But it is unlikely that you priced the *Asda* product so cheaply, and the *Rembrandt* brand so highly.

Which is the biggest selling toothpaste in the UK? *Colgate,* of course. So why don't we buy the *Asda* toothpaste when it is $1/5^{th}$ of the cost? The reason is that we trust *Colgate*. It is a leading brand. And quite frankly, the *Asda* product is so cheap it can't be any good, can it? Well, you don't know, because you have never tried it!

This illustrates the dynamics of price perception and value. If it's too cheap the product can become undermined.

So what about *Green People*? It is 3 times more expensive than *Colgate* and, in my humble opinion, it tastes awful! So why buy it? Well, because now the purchase isn't just about cleaning teeth. It's now about the environment and, for many people, it is worth paying a premium if a product is green.

And then we come to *Rembrandt*. "£8.49 for a tube of toothpaste!", I hear you cry. But one thing is for sure, it has got your interest because it is so expensive! This illustrates another dynamic of value. A high price will give a product status. The higher the price, the higher the desirability. All it then has to do is prove that it is value for money.

You can buy 8 tubes of *Colgate* for the price of one tube of *Rembrandt*. So why do people buy *Rembrandt*? Does it really clean your teeth 8 times better than *Colgate*? It doesn't have to. Walking through Times Square in New York I saw a 50-foot neon sign advertising *Rembrandt*. The advertising hoarding had nothing on it but their logo and two beautiful models with perfect teeth. They both looked... well, perfect! It confirmed that Rembrandt isn't just toothpaste, it's a lifestyle. And people are prepared to pay for lifestyle.

Never Negotiate Until Sold

There is an old adage that says "turnover is vanity, profit is sanity." Yet all too often salespeople start to lower the price or give things away just to chase the revenue. Indeed, they often do this despite the price not being the problem. In most cases, it was the solution match that was out of line.

Single Principled Salespeople never negotiate until 'sold', i.e. the buyer is convinced that they have a *compelling need* that is met by a *credible solution*. Only once they have agreement their product is a good match do they go to work on negotiating the package (see Figure 12).

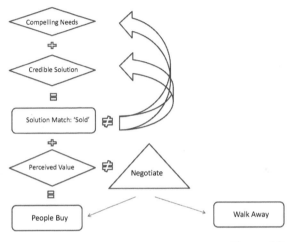

Figure 12

When negotiating, the Single Principled Salesperson ensures that the deal is 'win-win' for both parties. If they can't agree a solution they are prepared to walk away as 'win-lose' deals always end up being 'lose-lose' in the long-term.

The Buyer Myth

But listen to buyers and you really do believe that money talks. Buyers are a brutal species, taking sheer delight in making a salesperson sweat on price. They trick them into thinking it is all about cost, and if the salesperson doesn't drop their price they will find a supplier who will. Indeed, I think that some buyers actually believe in this hype themselves.

I thought this too. An old boss once made the mistake of telling me the minimum price I could sell at. From that day on, I would tentatively pitch a higher price, but in the back of my mind I always knew that I could discount. The minute the buyer 'erred' I would immediately drop my price. The funny thing was, although I would always undercut the incumbent, I rarely got the business. I couldn't work it out. I was cheaper, and the product I was supplying did the job just as well as theirs did. So how come they didn't buy?

The answer was the incumbent was proving better *value* for money than I was. They had a proven delivery record. I didn't. They had shown they could respond to urgent requests. I hadn't. They could call upon years of loyal service. I couldn't.

Here's the point:

Money may talk, but value speaks volumes.
You will never lose a deal on price, only on value.

I realised at that point that selling was about adding value, not reducing price. People buy what the product will do for them, not because of how much it costs. More significantly, they buy what they *perceive* the product will do for them. Perceived value is more important than actual value. Sometimes the value being offered may feel pretty intangible, but it is often the emotional buying motives rather than the rational motives that will dictate the value placed on the product.

I buy my meat from a local butcher for a number of reasons. Firstly, I perceive it to be of a better quality than the supermarket. I actually don't know if it is, but this perception means I am happy to pay more for it. I also perceive that the local butcher needs my business more than the supermarket. For all I know he may be a millionaire who doesn't need to work. I don't know, because I have never asked him. But in thinking that I am supporting my local community, I am happy to pay a premium.

Perceived Value

The Value Line graph in Figure 13 shows the correlation between price and the solution match.

If the price meets the solution match at the value line, the customer will perceive that they are receiving value for money. When price and solution match meet below the value line, the product/service is not delivering perceived value. Conversely, if they meet above the value line, perception of value is exceeded.

Mark Blackmore

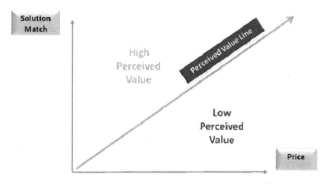

Figure 13

To illustrate the point, let me ask you: how much do you pay for a hair- cut? If you are male the answer will range from £5 in the local barber shop, to £75 in a high street brand such as Toni & Guy (see Figure 14).

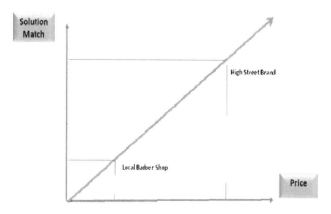

Figure 14

To understand the value being offered, let's compare them:

Local Barber Shop £5 - £15	High Street Brand Salon £35 –£75
Cut Neck razor Magazines & newspapers Gel	Appointment time slot Consultation Cappuccino/beer/wine Magazines & newspapers Hair wash & conditioner Head massage Cut Blow-dry Neck razor Gel Advice on hair products Stylish and highly-trained staff

Both establishments cut hair, but they offer very different solutions. Customers will only return if they feel they have been given value for money. Assuming both solutions give a good cut, the extra price is justified by offering a more sophisticated solution to meet the additional needs of the customer.

The Fall and Rise of M&S

When Stuart Rose took over Marks & Spencer in May 2004 the once jewel in Britain's high street was looking old-fashioned and tired. The products were still relatively high-priced, but the clothes looked like something your granny would buy! The British public expected more. When plotted on the value line graph, M&S clothing was falling way below the value line.

Stuart Rose had two options to get them back onto the line (see Figure 15).

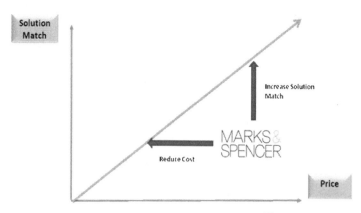

Figure 15

One option was to reduce the price. In doing so the products would have offered increased value, but the margins would also have been slashed. The other option open to Rose was to increase the perception of the M&S solution to meet the public's changing need.

His main line of attack was the latter. M&S hired top designers and beefed up their advertising with stylish celebrities (e.g. Twiggy, Myleen Klass, Take That). It worked. The share price grew from 350p In May 2004 to over 750p in just 3 years.

The Value Line Graph is a useful tool in assessing perceived value. If your product is falling below the line, or your competitors are above the line, you have to either reduce cost or increase the perception of the solution match. Reducing cost should always be the last resort. Increasing the perception of the solution match will ensure that you can justifiably charge premium prices.

Building Perceived Value

Perceived value is built by developing a rational and emotional 'needs bank' and selling the benefits of your solution.

The car industry is the master at creating perceived value. There are many types of car on the market that carry different price tags. All cars get you from A to B. But if it was just about that we would all be driving around in budget brands.

The car you buy will depend on how your emotional and rational buying motives are matched by the solution cost, as the illustration below demonstrates (see Figure 16).

Figure 16

If I only want convenience and independence I could probably buy a car for £1000. If I want it to be reliable, however, I probably need to spend a bit more. If I require even more guarantee in the form of warranties, I have to buy new and the price then starts to cost over the £10k mark. And if I want to impress the Joneses I need to spend much bigger bucks altogether.

Solutions come at a price, and not only in terms of money (see Figure 17). Other factors affecting the cost of your solution may be risk of change or hassle in moving to a new product/supplier.

Figure 17

For example, you are thirsty and want that bottle of water in the vending machine. But when you see the inflated price your natural reaction is to reject it. The cost of the solution has initially outweighed the need. You then realise, however, that there isn't anywhere else locally that sells water, and you think twice. This is because as well as being thirsty, you also want convenience. You buy the water, as the needs now outweigh the cost of the solution.

Salespeople generally spend very little time identifying needs. Eager to pounce on the first buying signal that is indicated to them, they present the solution as soon as they have established a slight interest. They then spend the rest of the call handling objections as the buyer feels that the solution isn't offering good value.

Like an expert batsman, the Single Principled Salesperson builds their innings by establishing a Needs Bank. Slashing out at the first ball of the over may result in a six, but they understand that, more often than not, it will send them walking straight back to the pavilion. Similarly, matching the first need with a solution may result in a sale, but they could have achieved an even bigger sale if they had more justification with stronger needs.

Variables – Protecting your Margins

We all like to get a good deal. It feels good. Single Principled Salespeople understand this and ensure that they achieve a feel-good factor by building *variables* into their sale. A variable is something that costs the salesperson very little, but has a perceived value to the customer.

Single Principled Salespeople are able to give the variable away without affecting their margin, whilst the customer gets 'something for nothing'. The result is win-win for both parties.

I was once sold a mobile phone contract and, like most buyers, I wanted to see how good a deal I could get. The phone I needed was a new model, and I knew that it was expensive to buy, even to retailers. I assumed there would be a charge for the phone, but within a few minutes of the pitch, the salesperson had given it away! When we arrived at the close I asked for a deal. He told me that he had already given me a good deal by throwing in a free phone. I reminded him that as far as I was concerned it was just part of the package he had presented, and *now* we needed to negotiate! Poor guy. He gave me a hands-free car kit to keep me quiet.

So what are the best variables?

Good variables are those that cost you little but have a high perceived value to the client. Bad variables are those that are expensive to you and/or have a low perceived value to the client. If it is high in cost to you it is eroding your gross margin. If it is low perceived value to the customer it isn't worth anything anyway!

Example:

We worked with an advertising company who identified the following variables:

Variable	Actual Cost to You High/Low	Perceived Benefit to Customer High/Low
Discount	High	High
Free Artwork	*Low*	*High*
Free Ads	High	High
Promotional Pens, etc	Low	Low
Payment Terms	High	High
Exclusivity	High	High
Page Position	*Low*	*High*

Based on their analysis, the best variables to give away were free artwork and page position as these were of low cost to them, but high *perceived value* to the customer. The salespeople previously were giving these away without attaching any value to them. In doing so, the only variables left with which to negotiate were discounts and free ads, which were of high cost. We changed all that. The salespeople now demonstrate value by positioning the cost of the variables, and giving away in priority of low cost to high.

Building Value in a Client Relationship

Value perception relates not only to the 'sale' but also applies to your overall relationship with the client. The higher up the relationship food chain you are, the more the client will value your product, service and opinion, and less emphasis will be placed on price.

There are 4 levels of relationship in the 'Relationship Pyramid' (see Figure 18):

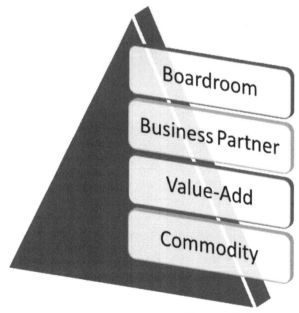

Figure 18

Level 1 – Commodity

There are lots of vendors who fall into this category. This is where the customer sees the supplier as simply the source of the product, and nothing more. If another organisation can provide the same product at a cheaper price they would more than likely buy from them instead.

Level 2 – Value-Add

This supplier is adding *perceived value*. This may be exceptional service, or providing a product that is unrivalled. The customer is more likely to continue to use a 'value-add' supplier than with the fickle relationship of a commodity supplier.

Level 3 – Business Partner

A partnership is formed between a client and vendor when the supplier is seen as a trusted advisor. The two companies are likely to work on joint projects together. There are much fewer Business Partner vendors than Value-add and Commodity vendors.

Level 4 – Boardroom

At this point the vendor has moved from a trusted advisor into, effectively, a 'non-executive director' role. The 'Big 4' consultancy firms often have this type of relationship, whereby key strategic decisions affecting the whole company are made with the supplier.

Single Principled Salespeople understand the value of clients perceiving them at a high level in the Relationship Pyramid. By being customer- focused, not self-focused, their sale becomes consultative. In doing so, they automatically elevate themselves in terms of building a stronger relationship with the client.

Mark Blackmore

Answers to Toothpaste challenge (all 50ml):

Asda 21p; Colgate £1.09; Green People £3.25; Rembrandt Plus £8.49 (Aug 2010 prices)

60 Second Summary:
Ensure Perceived Value

Money talks, but value speaks volumes. You will never lose a deal on price, only value.

Too many salespeople start to negotiate before they have even confirmed that their product/service matches the customer's need. The Single Principled Salesperson never negotiates until sold, i.e. the customer is sold on the product matching their needs. People then buy because they perceive that their compelling need is greater than the cost of the solution.

The Value Line Graph shows the correlation between price and solution match. If the value and solution match meet at the value line, the customer will perceive it to be value for money.

Perceived value is built by developing a rational and emotional needs bank and then pitching the credible solution.

Solutions come at a price, and not only in terms of money. Other factors affecting the cost of your solution may be risk of change, hassle in moving to a new supplier and/or loyalty.

A variable is something that can be used in a negotiation. A good variable is one that costs the salesperson very little, but has a perceived value to the customer.

Single Principled Salespeople are able to protect their margins by giving the customer 'something for nothing' (i.e. high perceived value/low cost variables). The result is win-win for both parties. The higher up the Relationship Pyramid you are, the more the client will value your product, service and opinion, and less emphasis will be placed on price.

Worksheet: Ensure Perceived Value

1. Value Line

Honestly plot where you and your competitors sit on the Value Line:

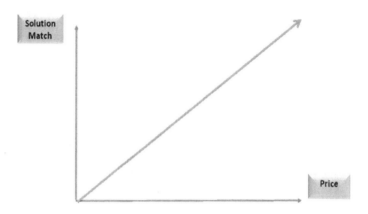

2. Adding Value

How can you add more value and move north on the value line?

_____
_____
_____
_____
_____
_____
_____

3. Variables

Write down the variables that you have to offer, and analyse their cost to you and perceived benefit to the customer.

Variable	Actual Cost to You *High/Low*	Perceived Benefit to Customer *High/Low*

4. Relationship Pyramid

Plot the relationships that you have with your top 10 clients on the pyramid below.

What can you do to elevate your company up the Relationship Pyramid?

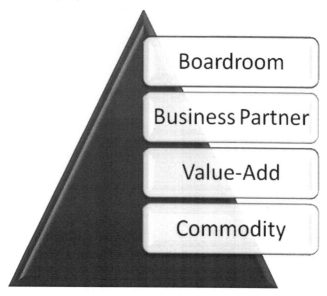

SUMMARY:
The 8th Myth of Selling

Summary
Exposing Sales Myth #8:
Fail to Plan, Plan to Fail

"Begin with the end in mind"

Dr Stephen Covey

Highly effective people 'begin with the end in mind', according to Dr Stephen Covey in his seminal book 'The 7 Habits of Highly Effective People.' And so we reach the conclusion of this book, and the 8th myth of selling: 'Fail to Plan, Plan to Fail.' For me, this myth sits apart from the other 7 myths as it has most truth in it. Yet it is probably the culprit of more unproductive sales hours than any other.

To understand the 8th myth you need to understand the fundamentals of the Single Sales Principle®, and the essence of the DECIDE® Sales Process. And it is for this reason that I have left the 8th myth until the end. To understand what to plan at the beginning of a sale, you need to understand what you are trying to achieve at the end of it.

Salespeople tend to fall into two camps: those who plan too much and those who hardly plan at all.

Those who plan too much tend to be 'busy fools,' i.e. running around doing very little. When we go out with these salespeople on calls they show us all the planning they have done: a tour of the client's website; the previous history; a list of questions they are going to ask; competitor information; marketing data, etc. The problem is, once they get into the sales meeting they don't even refer to it! Maybe being prepared makes the salesperson feel more secure and confident, a bit like a child's 'blanky'. But the bottom line is they really are wasting their time.

Pareto came up with the 80/20 rule, i.e. 80% of your results will come from 20% of your effort. For example: 80% of your turnover is likely to come from 20% of your customers; 80% of your bad debt will come from 20% of your client base, etc. And to this end, 80% of your effectiveness will come from 20% of your planning effort. The rest will be the icing on the cake.

Which leads us neatly onto the second camp: those salespeople who do very little planning. The fact is most salespeople fall into this category. You may be surprised to learn that so do Single Principled Salespeople.

"Hooray!" I hear the cry from the sales community at large. "What? No need to plan?"

Not quite! The difference with Single Principled Salespeople is that they 'begin with the end in mind.'

Imagine I were to throw £36.50 into the air. The money is made up of a £20, £10 and £5 note, and a £1 and 50p coin. There are two of you, and the person who grabs the most amount of money takes all of it. What would be your strategy? Here are some of the options you may consider:

- Take out the other guy and then grab as much as you can
- Use a net to gather up as much as possible in one swoop
- Jump start the gun

All would be great strategies providing you do one thing – you get the £20 note! The £20 is the key to winning the game. Whoever grabs the £20 wins regardless of what else is picked up. You may look busy gathering up the other notes and coins, but they are just 'noise.'

This demonstrates the theory put forward by Peter Drucker, the management guru, when he defined the difference between being 'effective' and being 'efficient':

"Efficiency is *doing things right*; Effectiveness is *doing the right things*."

The £20 is the right thing. It is the effective thing. In fact, it is the only thing.

We spend so much time doing things that look productive, but are just 'straight-lining.'

Straight-lining is my term for the art of making everything on your desk look symmetrical, because that's how 'organised people' look. Single Principled Salespeople are effective because they identify the '£20 notes.' It's why they often work fewer hours than the average performers.

The cartoonist, Doug Larson, said on time management, "For disappearing acts, it's hard to beat what happens to the eight hours supposedly left after eight of sleep and eight of

Mark Blackmore

work." I think we can all empathise with this sentiment. Life is too short to be planning for the sake of it.

So what are the *right things* to plan? From time to time I come across planning checklists that prompt the salesperson to remember all kinds of things, such as pen, rate card, order forms, etc. You shouldn't need a reminder to bring this. You do that anyway. It's no different from leaving the house and checking you have your wallet, keys and phone. It's a given.

When planning an account, Single Principled Salespeople simply put themselves in the buyer's shoes. They question why the customer should buy. And if they can't come up with a truly compelling answer they cancel the meeting/phone-call because they know they are only going to waste the buyer's time.

Planning to Win

The key to effective planning is to think about the Single Sales Principle® and pre-empt why the customer will buy:

a) Compelling Needs

'What *information* do I need to gather, and what are my qualification criteria?' (*IQ Questions*)

'What are the *rational* and *emotional buying motives* that will make my solution relevant?'

'What is my *value proposition*?'

'Which *pain/gain questions* do I need to ask that will identify *compelling needs*?'

b) Credible Solution

'What is my *credibility statement*?'

'How can I make my presentation *sizzle*?'

'What *proof* do I have that my product/service works?'

'What *case studies* do I have that are relevant to this situation?'

'Which *analogies* will illuminate my proposition?'

'Can I back up my claim with *killer statistics*?'

'Which *visual aids* will best represent my proposition?'

'Is there an opportunity to use the *sketchbook* technique?'

c) Perceived Value

'Where does my proposal fit on the *Value Line graph*?'

'How does my price\package compare to the competition?'

'Which *variables* can I introduce to the package?'

'Where does our current relationship sit on the *Relationship Pyramid*?'

'How can I improve the relationship?'

The Definition of Success

Mel Bernstein, the Miami narcotics detective played by Harris Yulin in the film *Scarface*, had a very simplistic view of success when he said: "Every day above ground is a good day!"

Many salespeople ask me on our programmes: "What is the definition of sales success?". My view is as simplistic as Bernstein's. The sale is successful when a customer's *compelling need* has been met by a *credible solution* that offers *perceived value*. In other words, the achievement of the Single Sales Principle®. That's it. If these elements have been achieved the sale has been a success.

They often reply to this: "But what if I hardly did anything at all? What if I just got lucky? What if they simply wanted to buy it? Have I still been a successful salesperson?"

My answer is a categorical YES! A sales process is just a vehicle to achieving the Single Sales Principle®. The method that we use at Lammore Consulting Ltd is the DECIDE® sales process. DECIDE® was created by understanding the exact requirements needed to fulfil the Single Sales Principle®. There are other processes available to use (although we would argue none achieves the Single Sales Principle® as well as ours, of course!). But, fundamentally, the vehicle used is not important. The result is all that matters. Success depends on the achievement of the Single Sales Principle®, regardless of how it is achieved.

I recently bought a new television. I had spent a lot of time researching on the internet and knew exactly the TV make and model (credible solution) to suit our functionality requirements and living room space (compelling needs). I had a good idea of the deals on offer, so when I walked into the electrical retail store all I was interested in was whether they would offer me perceived value over and above their competition. In just a few minutes I walked away as the proud owner of a new 32" flat-screen HD TV. You could argue that the salesperson didn't do anything to earn the sale. But you would be wrong. If she had gone through a full sales pitch she would have killed the sale. Remember: Single Principled Salespeople make it easy to buy. She did, however, offer me a really good deal, which was all that was needed to complete the Single Sales Principle®.

Actually, thinking about it, she did follow the DECIDE® method, but she used it to sell me the extended warranty. I usually never buy extended warranty. Despite always being asked, my standard reply to their half-hearted request is a polite "No, thank you." But this Single Principled Salesperson was different!

As I was at the till paying for the TV she asked if I had children, and how old they were. I explained they were pretty young and she mentioned that it was important to be aware that grubby, probing hands could damage the liquid crystals within the screen, rendering the whole thing unwatchable. In less than 30 seconds she identified a *compelling need*. The warranty was the *credible solution*. It happened also to be on special promotion, which offered *perceived value*. Hey presto, I bought the warranty!

I have no doubt that this salesperson hit her extended warranty target that week. Indeed, I bet she hits all of her targets every week! And this is the point. She clearly understands the importance of the Single Sales Principle®. And she knows how to achieve it.

And Finally

At the very beginning of this book I stated that: "Selling is the simplest of all professions. It follows a simple formula; a single principle." I stand by this claim, and unless you're the sort of person that reads a book from back to front, hopefully by now, so do you.

The simple principle I was referring to is, of course, the Single Sales Principle®. If you focus on matching *compelling needs* with *credible solutions* that offer *perceived value* you will succeed in selling. I guarantee it. Follow the 8 myths and you will become frustrated and disillusioned with our wonderful profession.

And it is indeed a wonderful profession. I am proud to be called a salesperson. And to all of those Single Principled Salespeople amongst you, I salute you.

Glossary

3 Phrase Rule: Never delivering more than three phrases at the start of a cold call without asking a question

30 Second Case Study Value Proposition: A very brief (approximately 30 seconds) overview of how you provided a credible solution to another organisation's compelling need

Bridging Question: The question that guides the sales call from 'Establish Credibility' into 'Confirm Opportunity'

Compelling Need: A problem or desire that motivates an individual into action

Confirm Opportunity: The third step of DECIDE®, used to identify essential information and qualify the potential of the sale

Conversation Opener: The initial question used to start a dialogue with a customer when making a cold call

Credibility Statement: The sequence of phrases used to introduce yourself and open up the client

Credible Solution: Matching a compelling need with the right product, supplied by the right vendor

Customer-Centric: Focusing on the customer's needs

DECIDE®: Lammore's sales methodology used to achieve the Single Sales Principle®

Define Value Proposition: The planning and first step of DECIDE®, used to focus on why the customer should buy

Demonstrate Proposition: The penultimate step of DECIDE®, used to engage the customer by showing them how the product/service meets their compelling needs

Emotional Buying Motive: An emotive reason for needing a product

Ensure Perceived Value: The last step of DECIDE®, used to 'close' the sale by confirming that the customer perceives the proposal is value for money

Establish Credibility: The second step of DECIDE®, used at the beginning of a sales call to introduce yourself by grabbing attention and creating interest

Ests: Unique selling points about your product/service

Gatekeeper: The person (e.g. secretary/P.A.) who stands between you and the decision-maker

Identify Compelling Needs: The fourth step of DECIDE®, used to establish emotional and rational buying motives that will motivate a customer into action

IQ Questions: Questions that identify essential information and qualify the opportunity

Killer Stats: Statistics that provide evidence that your proposition is credible

Needs Bank: Stacking up a number of compelling needs

Pain/Gain Questions: Questions used to test the extent to which a need is compelling by asking the consequence of *not* solving the need, or the benefit *of* solving it.

Passive Need: A need that does *not* motivate a customer into action, unlike a compelling need

Perceived Value: Occurs when the solution match and price are aligned

Proposition Concept: What a product does, how it meets the customer's needs, and why it does it better than any other method

Proposition Edge: Why your product delivers the proposition concept better than your competitors

Rational Buying Motive: A logical reason for needing a product

Relationship Pyramid: Defines the level of relationship a vendor has with the client

Sales-Centric: Focusing on the salesperson's agenda

Single Principled Salesperson: A salesperson who understands and focuses on the achievement of the Single Sales Principle®

Single Sales Principle®: People buy when a compelling need is met by a credible solution that offers perceived value

Sizzle Selling: The use of presentation techniques to engage the buyer and increase the impact of a presentation

Sketchbook: The technique of using a blank piece of paper to make a presentation

Solution Match: The credible solution required to meet the compelling needs of a customer

Straight-lining: Looking busy but not being effective

Value Line: The point at which the price meets the solution match

Value Proposition: A vendor's generic credible solution to meet the most likely compelling needs of a customer

Variables: The components that make up an offer/deal